GROWING INDEPENDENT

A Complementary Workbook to
A Journey to Independence

Second Edition

Tiffani Harvey

Written Words Publishing LLC
14189 E Dickinson Drive, Unit F
Aurora, Colorado 80014
www.writtenwordspublishing.com

Growing Independent © 2015 by Tiffani Harvey
Second Edition

Published by Written Words Publishing LLC August 31, 2023

ISBN: 978-1-961610-07-1 (paperback)
ISBN: 978-1-961610-08-8 (eBook)

Library of Congress Control Number: 2023914304

Cover Designed by Written Words Publishing LLC

Manufactured and printed in the United States of America

Table of Contents

Acknowledgements

This workbook was made possible because of Greg Falk. I would like to take this opportunity to thank Greg for his insight. In "A Journey to Independence," I ask a lot of questions, but I left no room to answer the questions. I was too far along to go back and put the needed spaces in, so I just started from scratch and made a workbook to go along with my story or to work as a standalone!

Of course, this book would never have been made if it wasn't for the grace and mercy of our wonderful Lord, the Author of Life.

Foreword

Growing Independent is a book of questions for the reader to use as a guide with a little information, definitions and examples. The reader is encouraged to think of their own questions to ask and to decide if the questions the author suggests are good questions for them to ask.

This book has the ideas and personal opinions of the author and the reader has the choice to agree or disagree with some or all of *Growing Independent*.

The readers of *Growing Independent* are responsible for their own actions and behaviors in relation to application and use of the book's content. The author does not claim responsibility, liability, loss, or risk, directly or indirectly.

Introduction

Growing Independent is a workbook to let your doctors, caregivers, guardians, and others know what your likes and dislikes are. This workbook gives you the chance to tell others why you like and dislike different things.

This workbook covers many subjects from who your professionals are to what your values are such as religious, political, multicultural, etc. It also covers various ways of life such as entertainment, your habits, how you like to communicate with others, how you handle your money, and more.

A question you will be asked many times is, "Why or why not or what do you need to find out to make an informed choice?" The reason for this question is to help *you* know yourself better and to help your personal and professional team support and protect you and your values.

In the author's opinion, it's easier to support and help someone when you understand why he or she likes or dislikes things. It's nice to know how much a person likes or dislikes things.

I'm going to ask three questions and answer each question as if each question had, "Why, why not or what do you need to find out to make a choice?"

An example is, "Do you want a cell phone?" "Yes, I do." "Why, why not or what do you need to find out to make a choice?" "I love to talk on the phone. I do as much business as I can while I'm on the road, so I can spend more time with my family."

"Do I want cable TV?" "No." "Why, why not or what do you need to find out to make a choice?" "Watching TV is a waste of my time, so paying for cable would be a waste of money."

If someone calls and asks, "Will you support us politically?" My answer is, "I don't know." "Why, why not or what do you need to find out to make a choice" "I need to know who they are and what kind of support they are asking for? If they need money, how will it be spent?"

Now that I've shown you how to answer the question, "Why, why not or what do you need to find out to make a choice?" you will know how to answer this question.

Finally, know your priorities. This is important, so if you have religious, family, employment, or college responsibilities at the same time, you will know what to do first, second, third, etc. For example, it is against some people's religion to work a certain day of the week, depending on their particular religion.

Protecting Yourself

Here's a list of terms and simple definitions:

"Wise," "being wise," or "wisdom" (in the context of this book) means having the time to gain knowledge and experience to help you make choices from a larger range of knowledge and experience when learned.

"Good choice" is a choice that keeps you healthy and safe, but you do not understand why or how the choice keeps you healthy or safe. (For example, you may choose to be a nonsmoker because it stinks. That's good, but if you don't understand the health risks or health benefits to smoking, you don't have wisdom.)

"Knowledge" means having the facts in your head. "Gaining knowledge" means the process of getting this knowledge. We can have knowledge without experience. (For example, "Don't touch the stove!") Hopefully, you've never had the experience of touching a hot stove, but if you know in your head to *never* touch a hot stove, you have knowledge!

"Understanding" means knowing what the consequences of your choices are: whether they are good or bad.

It is important to listen to other people and find out what other people say on any subject. Find out if it's a fact or their opinion. The way to tell if something is a fact or an opinion is to ask, "Where did you get your information from?" If the person cannot tell you, it's probably an opinion. Keep an open mind. Find out how many people have that opinion.

When possible, find some facts *before* you make a choice about anything!

To know the difference between wisdom and opinion, take what is said with a grain of salt. If lots of people say the same thing, it's probably worth it to look into it as a fact or a smart opinion for consideration.

For example, pregnant women drinking—some people may tell you their religious or moral beliefs or opinions, and other people may tell you their medical knowledge, and some people may think drinking is okay as long as a woman is not pregnant, etc.

Develop your own opinions on every topic but be open to logic and reason. *Be willing to change your opinion when someone gives you a reason or reasons to change your mind on any subject!*

"Experience" means the knowledge gained by having done something in the past. (For example: At age 10, I saw two $1 lottery tickets on the ground. My mom asked me, "Do you want to buy two more lottery tickets or do you want me to cash in the $2 and give it to you?" This was my mom's way of teaching me a lesson about gambling so I would stop looking at the fast, easy money and take the *time* to watch and learn!) Regarding the hot stove: If you touch a hot stove, you learn from experience not to touch it again.

Do you think we won any more money or lost the $2 we bought the tickets with? We lost the $2 and we didn't buy anymore! That was my *experience* with gambling!

"Foolish" means making a bad choice because you didn't ask anyone with knowledge or experience before making the choice.

A foolish person refuses to ask for advice from someone who has the knowledge, understanding, and experience to help them gain knowledge and understanding such as, "What does someone need to know and understand to be and stay safe?" A foolish person will also ignore other's advice.

"Bad choice" is often a foolish choice. It's made when you don't understand all the results of the choice you made.

"Wrong choice" means choosing to do something that is against the law or choosing to do something that hurts someone else or you so badly that someone dies or can't recover.

Making choices that others would consider foolish or bad are okay. If you *learn* from your mistakes and the mistakes of others, you will become wiser.

IF YOU NEVER MAKE A MISTAKE, YOU WILL NEVER GAIN EXPERIENCE OR LEARN FROM YOUR MISTAKES.

Personal Information

Name: _____

Date: _____

Address: _____

_____

Date of Birth: _____

Day Phone: _____

Evening Phone: _____

Cell Phone: _____

Email: _____

Trusted People: _____

_____

Trusted people give you advice to help you make your own choices!

Trusted people can be anyone you trust; however, a guardian and standby guardian shouldn't be one of the trusted people because they have to make final choices. A Power of Attorney might be okay because they are someone you chose to make final choices. (A spring Power of Attorney has power only when a person becomes incompetent or incapacitated.)

(Most of the time I will use "Power of Attorney." I'm using the term "Power of Attorney" for all kinds of the final authority because there are many different kinds of Power of Attorney.)

Who are your family members and friends that you want to help you to make final decisions or choices?

_____

_____

Do you want to give your opinions to another person and have that person make the final choice? (Circle one)

___ Yes ___ No ___ Maybe ___ Don't Know

Who do you want to make the final decisions or choices over your everyday choices in life if you are unable or do not want to speak for yourself? (List in order who you want these people to be.) If you don't know, take a separate sheet of paper and write a list of everyone you trust. List the good things and the bad things of each person, then narrow it down to the three people you trust most.

1. _____

2. _____

3. _____

If you don't know the names, addresses, or phone numbers of any of the professionals in following questions, leave the space blank.

Power of Attorney

Name: _____

Job Title: _____

Address: _____

_____

Phone: _____

Email: _____

Guardian

Name: _____

Job Title: _____

Address: _____

_____

Phone: _____

Email: _____

Alternative POA #1

Name: _____

Job Title: _____

Address: _____

_____

Phone: _____

Email: _____

Alternative POA #2

Name: _____

Job Title: _____

Address: _____

_____

Phone: _____

Email: _____

Advocate

Name: _____

Address: _____

_____

Phone: _____

Email: _____

Advocate

Name: _____

Address: _____

_____

Phone: _____

Email: _____

Doctor M.D.

Name: _____

Address: _____

_____

Phone: _____

Email: _____

Dentist

Name: _____

Address: _____

_____

Phone: _____

Email: _____

Eye Doctor

Name: _____

Address: _____

_____

Phone: _____

Email: _____

Special Doctor

Name: _____

Address: _____

_____

Phone: _____

Email: _____

Special Doctor

Name: _____

Address: _____

_____

Phone: _____

Email: _____

Special Doctor

Name: _____

Address: _____

_____

Phone: _____

Email: _____

Social Worker

Name: _____

Address: _____

_____

Phone: _____

Email: _____

Social Worker

Name: _____

Address: _____

_____

Phone: _____

Email: _____

Care Giving Agency

Name: _____

Address: _____

_____

Phone: _____

Email: _____

Case Manager

Name: _____

Address: _____

_____

Phone: _____

Email: _____

Other Professional

Name: _____

Address: _____

_____

Phone: _____

Email: _____

What kind of Power of Attorney or guardian do you have? If you have alternate Powers of Attorney or a standby guardian, write it here.

_____

_____

_____

_____

_____

_____

_____

_____

Medications

Your health is very, very important to those who love and know you personally. Your health is also important to me, to society, and to those who love you, such as your family and friends. It's important because they know you. I care about your health because I'm writing to a population who already suffers from disabilities. My goal is to help people with disabilities be as independent as possible. If medicine can help you, why avoid it? It's supposed to make you as healthy as possible! Your health is important to society because when people are healthy the taxpayers in society pay less money for healthcare. When people are unhealthy or sick, society pays more taxes for healthcare.

Here are a few questions to ask your doctor if you don't know the answers. If you know the answers, write it down and don't ask your doctor.

How is each medicine supposed to help you?

_____

_____

_____

Is each one of your medicines doing what it is supposed to do for you?

___ Yes ___ No ___ Some of Them ___ Don't Know

How?

_____

_____

How does the medicine you take help you?

_____

_____

_____

What are the side effects and risks of each medicine you are taking?

_____

_____

_____

If *you* are having side effects that you are not willing to live with or if the side effects to a medicine are worse than the reason you are taking it, talk to the doctor to see if he/she can change your medicine to a medicine with fewer side effects and find out if he/she has any other ideas of how to manage your medical/mental health problem other than prescription medicine.

What are other ways you can think of to manage your medical/mental health along with taking prescription medicine?

_____

_____

_____

Do you know what could happen to you if you don't take prescription medicine? Ask your doctor or pharmacist if you don't know.

___ Yes ___ No ___ Kind Of ___ Don't Know

15

If you don't want to take medicine, will you: (If you don't know, write what you need to find out about each idea so you can make a choice.)

Eat healthy?

___ Yes ___ No ___ Think About It ___ Don't Know

Take vitamins?

___ Yes ___ No ___ Think About It ___ Don't Know

Get counseling?

___ Yes ___ No ___ Think About It ___ Don't Know

Exercise often?

___ Yes ___ No ___ Think About It ___ Don't Know

Avoid foods that could increase the reason for taking medicine?

___ Yes ___ No ___ Think About It ___ Don't Know

Eat foods that could reduce the reason for taking the medicine?

___ Yes ___ No ___ Think About It ___ Don't Know

The following questions tell others what you want to be able to do yourself, what you need/want to learn so you can do it yourself, and what you need/want others to do for you.

Do you want to take *your own* medicine and vitamins?

___ Yes ___ No ___ Maybe
___ Need to Learn at Another Time

Do you want to make a plan to help you remember to take your medicines, vitamins, etc. every day?

___ Yes ___ No ___ Maybe ___ Don't Know

If yes, what's your plan? If maybe or don't know, what information do you need to find before making a decision?

_____

_____

_____

_____

Do you want to make a plan to let yourself know when you have already taken your medicines, vitamins, etc. so you won't accidently take too much medicine?

    ___ Yes ___ No

Do you want to make a plan to take the correct medicines, vitamins, etc. at the correct time of day?

    ___ Yes ___ No ___ Maybe ___ Don't Know

If yes, what's the plan? If maybe or don't know, what information do you need to find out to make an informed choice?

_____

_____

_____

_____

Do you need a plan to take the correct amount? This can be hard if the amount is different or at different times of the day. (For example, the doctors changed how much I was taking of each medication. Now, I take 1½ of my medication in the morning and two at night.) If you have a medication(s) with different instructions for day and night, would you be able to always remember those instructions?

    ___ Yes   ___ No

Who do you want to teach you or help you come up with a plan to safely take your medication??

_____

_____

_____

If you don't know who you want to teach you, what do you need to find out to make that decision?

_____

_____

_____

Who do you want to give you your medicines?

_____

If you don't know, what do you need to find out to make that decision?

_____

_____

_____

How do you want to get information from your pharmacy about your medications?

    ___ By Myself   ___ Someone Else   ___ Don't Know

If someone else, who?

_____

If you don't know, what do you need to find out to make that decision?

_____

_____

_____

"Informed consent" is a paper you sign *after* a doctor or nurse explains all the possible risks and what you should expect from what they give you such as medication or surgery. DON'T SIGN ANYTHING YOU DON'T UNDERSTAND!

Do you want to talk to your medical team or do you want someone else to do it? (These could be signing papers such as a release of information, "informed consent" papers, etc.)

_____ You   _____ Someone Else   _____ Don't Know

If someone else, who?

_____

Why did you choose that person (even if it's you)? If you don't know, what do you need to find out to make that decision?

_____

_____

_____

Personal Preferences

Do consider yourself to be religious?

___ Yes ___ No ___ Maybe ___ Don't Know

If yes, what is *your* faith/religion?

_____

Why did you choose that faith/religion?

_____

_____

_____

If no, are you looking for a faith/religion, a place of worship, or are you open to anyone talking to you about their faith/religion or where they attend worship services?

___ Yes ___ No ___ Maybe ___ Don't Know

Why or why not?_____

_____

_____

Are you registered to vote?

___ Yes ___ No ___ Don't Know

Being a registered voter does *not* mean you must vote! It means you have the choice to vote each time there is an election. If you are not registered to vote, you don't have the option. You cannot vote *before* you are registered!

If you are not registered to vote, do you want to be registered to vote?

___ Yes   ___ No   ___ Maybe   ___ Don't Know

Why or why not?_____

_____

_____

All Safety Issues:
What Is Your Comfort Zone?
What Do You Feel Safe With?

For these next few statements, what would you do? Are you comfortable:

Being alone in public? ___ Yes ___ No

Being in a group in public? ___ Yes ___ No

Does it change depending on the situation?

___ Yes ___ No

When you join a group, are you:

Comfortable watching others for the first few times?

___ Yes ___ No

Comfortable jumping into a conversation when it's your first time?

___ Yes ___ No

Are you both ways, depending on the group you are in?

___ Yes ___ No

Does it depend on the situation?

___ Yes ___ No

Communication/Conversation Opinions

What people say and how people say things can keep them and others safe or can put them and others in danger. Things people don't say can keep them and others safe or can put them and others in danger. Communication tells the world how you are thinking and feeling!

What is your opinion of another person doing most of the talking and not letting you talk very much?

_____

_____

_____

_____

_____

Do you like to talk nonstop and not allow the other person to talk very much?

____ Yes ____ No ____ Sometimes ____ Don't Know

What would you do if someone does not respond to you when you say, "Hi," "Hello," or "How are you?"

_____

_____

_____

_____

_____

Safe and Unsafe Conversations

How would you approach someone you want to talk to? What are things you could say?

_____

_____

_____

_____

How do you get the attention of a person who has a visual impairment if you don't know their name and you want to talk to them?

_____

_____

_____

_____

If you are shopping in the grocery store and someone bumps into you saying, "Oh, I'm sorry," is it appropriate for you to give them your name?

___ Yes ___ No ___ Sometimes
___ Maybe ___ Don't Know

Why or why not?_____

_____

_____

_____

When you ask or someone else asks you, "How are you," should one of you share a little about yourself and then should the other person share a little about themself?

___ Yes ___ No ___ Sometimes
___ Maybe ___ Don't Know

Why or why not?_____

_____

_____

_____

What do you consider to be safe topics? (Check all that apply.)

___ Food ___ Music ___ Sports ___ Religion
___ Weather ___ School ___ Employment
___ Politics ___ Other

Is it okay to ask a stranger, "How are you," if their body language is friendly?

___ Yes ___ No ___ Sometimes
___ Maybe ___ Don't Know

Why or why not?_____

_____

_____

_____

What do you consider to be unsafe topics of conversation? (Check all that apply.)

___ Food ___ Music ___ Sports ___ Religion
___ Weather ___ School ___ Employment
___ Politics ___ Other

Why do you consider these unsafe subjects/topics?

_____

_____

_____

_____

If someone makes a rude comment about someone with a disability, what should you do? (Check all that apply.)

___ Educate them

___ Just walk away

___ Leave the choice up to the person who has the disability (if the comment is directed at someone)

___ Ignore the comment 100% and keep talking to them as if you didn't hear what they said

If you choose to stop and educate that person, would you take the person's feelings into consideration?

___ Yes ___ No ___ Sometimes ___ It Depends
___ Maybe ___ Don't Know

Why or why not?_____

_____

_____

_____

When meeting someone new, are there subjects that you don't want to talk about?

___ Yes ___ No ___ Maybe ___ Don't Know

Why or why not?_____

_____

_____

If you answered yes or maybe, what are those subjects?

_____

_____

Do you think the person you are meeting has subjects they don't want to talk about?

___ Yes ___ No ___ Maybe ___ Don't Know

Why or why not?_____

_____

_____

How would you like people making comments about your looks, speech, or the way you walk, etc., if it was because of your disability?

___Like it ___ Dislike it ___ Not Sure ___ Don't Know

Why or why not?_____

_____

_____

Do you think it is right to make comments about the color of someone's skin?

___ Yes ___ No ___ Sometimes
___ Maybe ___ Don't Know

Why or why not?_____

_____

_____

Do you think it is okay to make comments about someone's gender? Gender means male or female.

    ___ Yes   ___ No   ___ Sometimes
    ___ Maybe   ___ Don't Know

Why or why not?_____

_____

_____

Do you think it is okay to make comments about someone's age?

    ___ Yes   ___ No   ___ Sometimes
    ___ Maybe   ___ Don't Know

Why or why not?_____

_____

_____

Personal Safety

When you are out in the public, knowing what to do and where to go if someone wants to hurt you is *very important*! It is important to have a plan before any possible problems come up!

The following ideas are put into the form of questions. Consider these ideas as ways to protect yourself! If you have any other ideas for staying safe, do those things and share them with others. (Please email your ideas to me at responsiblyindependent@yahoo.com.)

Do you want to take a self-defense class where they help you use your weaknesses or disabilities as an asset instead of a barrier?

____ Yes ____ No ____ Maybe ____ Don't Know

Why or why not?_____

_____

_____

_____

Do you need a cell phone for emergency purposes only?

____ Yes ____ No ____ Maybe ____ Don't Know

Why or why not?_____

_____

_____

_____

Name three reasons why you would call 911 on your cell phone.

1. _____

2. _____

3. _____

Do you want a cell phone for other safety reasons and other reasons?

___ Yes ___ No

If yes, what are those reasons? _____

_____

_____

_____

If no, why not? _____

_____

_____

_____

Do you think that talking to your advocates, trusted family members, friends, or power of attorney/guardian about other safety reasons is a good idea?

___ Yes ___ No ___ Maybe ___ Don't Know

Why or why not?_____

_____

_____

Name three safety reasons for owning a cell phone other than calling 911.

1. _____

2. _____

3. _____

If someone was following you or was doing something you told them to stop doing, would you report them to the police?

___ Yes   ___ No   ___ Maybe   ___ Don't Know

Why or why not?_____

_____

_____

If you choose to make a police report, you need to know the date, the time, and give as many details as possible.

Do you know *what* mace, pepper spray, or a zapper is used for? Answer Yes or No for each of the following:

Mace: ___ Yes   ___ No   ___ Want to Learn

What is mace? _____

_____

Pepper spray: ___ Yes   ___ No   ___ Want to Learn

What is pepper spray? _____

_____

Zapper: ___ Yes ___ No ___ Want to Learn

What is a zapper? _____

_____

Do you know *when* you are supposed to use each one of these devices?

Mace: ___ Yes ___ No ___ Want to Learn

When? _____

_____

Pepper spray: ___ Yes ___ No ___ Want to Learn

When? _____

_____

Zapper: ___ Yes ___ No ___ Want to Learn

When? _____

_____

Do you know *how* to use each one of the following devices? Answer yes or no for each.

Mace: ___ Yes ___ No ___ Want to Learn

How? _____

_____

Pepper Spray: ___ Yes ___ No ___ Want to Learn

How? _____

_____

Zapper: ___ Yes ___ No ___ Want to Learn

How? _____

_____

Think about doing any or all of the following suggestions to "act safe" even when you "feel unsafe," so you can "***stay safe***."

Would you walk with your head held high as if you know where you are going even if you are lost?

___ Yes ___ No ___ Sometimes
___ Maybe ___ Don't Know

Why or why not?_____

_____

_____

Would you walk a little faster even if you were just hanging out or in a hurry?

___ Yes ___ No ___ Sometimes
___ Maybe ___ Don't Know

Why or why not?_____

_____

_____

Would you walk fast if you thought you were in danger?

___ Yes ___ No ___ Sometimes
___ Maybe ___ Don't Know

Why or why not?_____

_____

_____

Would you want to look like you are walking with a specific place to go and as if you need to get there quickly (even if you don't)?

___ Yes ___ No ___ Sometimes
___ Maybe ___ Don't Know

Why or why not?_____

_____

_____

Do you think the suggestions listed above would help you be safer, not as safe, or equally as safe as you are now?

___ Safer ___ Not As Safe
___ Equally As Safe As You Are Now

Explain your opinion.

_____

_____

_____

_____

_____

Stranger Questions in General

Would you feel comfortable getting advice from a stranger?

___ Yes ___ No ___ Sometimes
___ Maybe ___ Don't Know

Why or why not?_____

_____

_____

Do you think it is appropriate to give advice to a stranger?

___ Yes ___ No ___ Sometimes
___ Maybe ___ Don't Know

Why or why not?_____

_____

_____

Do you think a stranger would feel comfortable getting advice from someone they don't know?

___ Yes ___ No ___ Sometimes
___ Maybe ___ Don't Know

Why or why not?_____

_____

_____

If a stranger comes up to you and asks you to do a favor for them, would you do it?

___ Yes ___ No ___ Sometimes
___ Maybe ___ Don't Know

Why or why not?_____

_____

_____

Would you go up to a stranger and ask them to do a favor for you?

___ Yes ___ No ___ Sometimes
___ Maybe ___ Don't Know

Why or why not?_____

_____

_____

Gossiping (Conversation Do Nots)

Gossiping is talking about someone who is not included in the conversation.

Are you or someone around you gossiping?

___ Yes ___ No

A good test would be to ask yourself, "Would I say it if they were listening?" Answer this question silently to yourself.

___ Yes ___ No ___ Maybe ___ Don't Know

If the answer is no, it is gossiping. If the answer is yes, it is not gossiping.

Here are two situations. Consider each situation and decide if it is gossiping.

Two college students were talking and one student said, "I work in the student government."

The other student said, "Oh, then you must know Angel."

The first student thought for a while and finally said, "So many students come through the office I can't remember her."

The second student gave some very specific physical descriptions of her, and the first student remembered who she was. "Oh yeah, she's real nice. She keeps us on our toes and fights for the disabled!"

The second student said, "That's my wife!"

Do you think that man would mind if the husband told his wife?

___ Yes ___ No ___ Maybe ___ Don't Know

Explain:_____

_____

_____

How do you think Angel felt when she heard it?

_____

_____

_____

A second example is, someone says, "She would look so much more professional and beautiful if she would just stop body piercing and putting tattoos all over herself!"

How would you feel if she heard you saying that and saw you pointing at her?

___ Embarrassed ___ Ashamed ___ Angry ___ Happy
___ Sad ___ Proud ___ Don't Know
Other _____

Why did you answer that way?

_____

_____

_____

How would you feel if someone gossips about you?

_____

_____

_____

If someone you know is gossiping to you about someone else, chances are that person is going to gossip about you to another person, maybe even to your friends.

Give four examples of gossiping to show that you understand what gossiping is.

1. _____

2. _____

3. _____

4. _____

If you found out a friend was gossiping to you about another friend, what would you do?

_____

_____

_____

_____

_____

Home and Neighborhood Safety

When you leave the house, do you lock the doors and windows?

___ Yes ___ No

Why or why not?_____

_____

_____

When you go to bed, do you lock the doors and windows?

___ Yes ___ No

Why or why not?_____

_____

_____

Timers on lights mean the lights are timed to turn on and off in different rooms in your home. As one light goes off, another light turns on a couple of seconds after the other light has turned off.

Do you want to get timers on your lights?

___ Yes ___ No ___ Maybe ___ Don't Know

Why or why not?_____

_____

_____

_____

If you are buying or own your home, this next question is especially for you:

Would you get a security alarm for your home?

___ Yes ___ No ___ Maybe ___ Don't Know

Why or why not?_____

_____

_____

_____

When walking down the street, would you walk against the traffic or with the traffic?

___ With ___ Against ___ Doesn't Matter to You
___ Don't Know

Why?_____

_____

_____

_____

When riding a bicycle down the street, would you ride with or against the traffic?

___ With ___ Against ___ Doesn't Matter to You
___ Don't Know

Why?_____

_____

_____

_____

Driving Strangers or Riding with Strangers Safety

Do you know what hitchhiking is?

___ Yes   ___ No   ___ Kind Of

If you answered "yes" or "kind of," what is hitchhiking?

_____

_____

_____

What is your opinion of hitchhiking?

___ Approve   ___ Disapprove   __ Not Sure
___ Don't Know

Why, why not and under what circumstances?

_____

_____

_____

Would you accept a ride from a stranger?

___ Yes   ___ No   ___ Sometimes
___ Maybe   ___ Don't Know

Why, why not and under what circumstances?

_____

_____

_____

Would you offer a ride to a stranger?

   ___ Yes ___ No ___ Sometimes
   ___ Maybe ___ Don't Know

Why, why not and under what circumstances?

_____

_____

_____

Would you feel safe riding alone with a stranger?

   ___ Yes ___ No ___ Sometimes
   ___ Maybe ___ Don't Know

Why, why not and under what circumstances?

_____

_____

_____

Would you feel comfortable giving a ride to a stranger?

   ___ Yes ___ No ___ Sometimes
   ___ Maybe ___ Don't Know

Why, why not and under what circumstances?

_____

_____

_____

Protecting Yourself from Stalking and Violence When Dating, Married or Living Together

The reason for writing the following story is to get you thinking about *where* you feel safe or unsafe meeting someone you would consider dating, living with, or marrying.

Basically, how long would you want to know someone in public before you exchange different kinds of personal information?

I never considered finding a spouse on public transportation, but that's how I met my husband. One day, I saw a boy in a wheelchair sitting in my favorite spot on the bus. I chose to sit in front of him, introduced myself, and started talking to him. His caregiver spoke up and helped him communicate. The boy was unable to speak. I kept running into the same boy and the same caregiver. Finally, I asked the caregiver two questions: "Don't you ever get a day off?" and "Why can't you remember my name?"

The answers were, "I'm not his caregiver. I'm his father. I'm blind. I can't see who is talking to me."

The father and I enjoyed the same kind of music, we both rode the city bus, and we also had similar hobbies. Finally, I heard the boy at church and went searching for him and his father. Our employment goals, some of our hobbies, and some of our political views were different, but we were able to accept each other's differences.

Talk to your support team about safety measures. Safety measures would be: How long do you want to know someone before you allow them in your space or before you give out your personal information? Know the kind of personalities you get along with and the ones you can't deal with. *Know yourself* well enough to answer the following questions, and if you can't answer all the questions, it would be smart to save dating, living together and marriage for later in the future.

Know yourself well enough to set your own boundaries. Know yourself well enough to know what *your* safety boundaries are. Safety boundaries include space and touch boundaries. If the two of you like enough of the same things to make a friendship into a special relationship, then the two of you need to establish what kind of relationship you have.

To check them out for safety, make a lot of copies of the following checklist and go through the checklist for each person you would consider having a close friendship with.

First of all, did you meet someone you would like to have a closer friendship with?

___ Yes ___ No

If yes, who?_____

For each new person in your life, go through the safety checklist:

Have they put you down with words?

___ Yes ___ No ___ Maybe ___ Don't Know

If yes, what have they said?

_____

_____

_____

Do you know if they have put others down with words?

___ Yes ___ No ___ Maybe ___ Don't Know

Do they limit the friends you can have?

___ Yes ___ No ___ Sometimes ___ Don't Know

If you don't know, what steps will you take to find out if they limit who you can have as friends?

_____

_____

_____

_____

_____

Under what situations do they limit or control how much contact you have with your family or friends?

_____

_____

_____

_____

Do they tell you when you can or can't go out?

___ Yes ___ No ___ Don't Know

How often?

___ Never ___ Rarely ___ Sometimes
___ Often ___ Always

Do they tell you when you have to be home?

___ Yes ___ No ___ Don't Know

How often?

   ___ Never   ___ Rarely   ___ Sometimes
   ___ Often   ___ Always

Do they tell you what time you are allowed to go out and what time to be home?

   ___ Yes   ___ No   ___ Don't Know

How often?

   ___ Never   ___ Rarely   ___ Sometimes
   ___ Often   ___ Always

Do they tell you where you can or can't go?

   ___ Yes   ___ No   ___ Don't Know

How often?

   ___ Never   ___ Rarely   ___ Sometimes
   ___ Often   ___ Always

Do they tell you who you can or can't call?

   ___ Yes   ___ No   ___ Don't Know

How often?

   ___ Never   ___ Rarely   ___ Sometimes
   ___ Often   ___ Always

Do they tell you for what reason(s) you can or can't go out?

   ___ Yes   ___ No   ___ Don't Know

How often?

   ___ Never   ___ Rarely   ___ Sometimes
   ___ Often   ___ Always

Do you ever feel unsafe with this person?

___ Yes ___ No ___ Maybe ___ Don't Know

How often?

___ Never ___ Rarely ___ Sometimes
___ Often ___ Always

Have they ever controlled anyone else that you know of?

___ Yes ___ No ___ Kind Of ___ Not Sure
___ Don't Know

Do they take your money without your permission?

___ Yes ___ No ___ Don't Know

How often?

___ Never ___ Rarely ___ Sometimes
___ Often ___ Always

Have they taken anyone else's money without them knowing?

___ Yes ___ No ___ Maybe ___ Don't Know

How often do they try to make you feel guilty on purpose?

___ Daily ___ Weekly ___ Biweekly
___ Monthly ___ Yearly

How often have they tried to make others feel guilty on purpose?

___ Daily ___ Weekly ___ Biweekly
___ Monthly ___ Yearly

Are they jealous of your time, energy or possessions?

___ Yes ___ No ___ Sometimes
___ Maybe ___ Don't Know

Has this person ever been jealous of anyone else's time, energy or possessions?

   ___ Yes   ___ No   ___ Sometimes
   ___ Maybe   ___ Don't Know

Has the person that you want to date or marry ever made you feel uncomfortable by trying to get information you don't want to share when they called and wanted to know what you were doing?

   ___ Yes   ___ No   ___ Don't Know

How often?

   ___ Never   ___ Rarely   ___ Sometimes
   ___ Often   ___ Always

(It's great to set boundaries, but it's up to every person how much information they want to share.)

Have they ever isolated you?

   ___ Yes   ___ No   ___ Don't Know
   ___ Never   ___ Rarely   ___ Sometimes   ___ Always

If yes, do you think it would be smart to break off contact?

   ___ Yes   ___ No

Do you know if they have ever isolated others?

   ___ Yes   ___ No   ___ Don't Know

How often?

   ___ Never   ___ Rarely   ___ Sometimes
   ___ Often   ___ Always

Do they have a history of physically abusing animals?

   ___ Yes   ___ No   ___ Maybe   ___ Don't Know

If you answered "maybe" or "don't know," how would you find out?

_____

_____

_____

Do they have a history of sexually abusing animals?

_____ Yes _____ No _____ Maybe _____ Don't Know

If you answered "maybe" or "don't know," how would you find out?

_____

_____

_____

Do they have a history of physically abusing children?

_____ Yes _____ No _____ Maybe _____ Don't Know

If you answered "maybe" or "don't know," how would you find out?

_____

_____

_____

Do they have a history of sexually abusing children?

_____ Yes _____ No _____ Maybe _____ Don't Know

If you answered "maybe" or "don't know," how would you find out?

_____

_____

_____

If the answer is "yes," "maybe," or "don't know" to any of the physical or sexual abuse questions, why would you want to be friends with, date, or marry that person?

_____

_____

_____

_____

_____

Have they destroyed your stuff?

_____ Yes _____ No _____ Maybe _____ Don't Know

Do you know if they have ever destroyed anyone else's stuff?

_____ Yes _____ No _____ Maybe _____ Don't Know

Some people argue all the time, others hate arguing. Some people are the peacemakers, and others like to cause trouble.

Do you like to be around peacemakers?

_____ Yes _____ No _____ Doesn't Matter _____ Don't Know

Do you like to be around troublemakers?

_____ Yes _____ No _____ Doesn't Matter _____ Don't Know

Do you like the kind of people who stir up trouble by fighting for good causes?

_____ Yes _____ No _____ Doesn't Matter _____ Don't Know

Do you like to be a peacemaker?

_____ Yes _____ No _____ Doesn't Matter _____ Don't Know

Do you like people with compassion?

_____ Yes _____ No _____ Doesn't Matter _____ Don't Know

Does the volume of someone's voice matter to you?

_____ Yes _____ No _____ Sometimes
_____ Depends on the Situation _____ Don't Know

If sometimes, when does volume bother you?

_____

_____

_____

Did you grow up with arguing all around you?

_____ Yes _____ No

Do you like constant arguing?

_____ Yes _____ No _____ Maybe _____ Don't Know

Why or why not?_____

_____

_____

Do you like to argue?

_____ Yes _____ No _____ Sometimes

How often?

   ___ Rarely   ___ Sometimes   ___ Often   ___ Always
   ___ Never

If arguing is a habit, would you like to break the habit or continue to argue?

   ___ Yes   ___ No   ___ Maybe   ___ Don't Know

Do you want to continue arguing in future relationships?

   ___ Yes   ___ No   ___ Maybe   ___ Don't Know

Why or why not?_____

_____

_____

Do they hold grudges?

   ___ Yes   ___ No   ___ Sometimes   ___ Don't Know

Do they make you feel guilty when you hurt their feelings or do they forgive you?

   ___ Guilty   ___ Forgiving   ___ Don't Know

Do you hold grudges against them or forgive them?

   ___ Grudges   ___ Forgiving   ___ Don't Know

Do you make others feel guilty when your feelings get hurt?

   ___ Yes   ___ No   ___ Sometimes   ___ Don't Know

Which kind of people do you like being around? (Check all that apply.)

   ___ A passive person
   ___ An assertive person
   ___ An aggressive person
   ___ A passive-aggressive person

Regarding the question above, everyone who cares about you should know why you choose to be like that. This should be *out of concern*, not control!

(I would want to get this information from my teenage son/daughter even if they don't have disabilities. If I knew nothing else about who my adult children were dating or going to marry, I would want to know why they were interested in the different types of people listed above.)

Do you like being around people who are sensitive to you?

___ Yes ___ No ___ Sometimes ___ Don't Know

Do you like being around people who are sensitive to others?

___ Yes ___ No ___ Sometimes ___ Don't Know

Do you like being around people who have a military-style personality?

___ Yes ___ No ___ Sometimes ___ Don't Know

If you are not sure about any of the above set of questions, what do you need to find out to decide?

_____

_____

_____

_____

Do the two of you share the same spiritual background?

___ Yes ___ No ___ Maybe ___ Don't Know

If not, does the other person respect your spiritual background or lack of?

___ Yes ___ No ___ Maybe ___ Don't Know

If not, why?_____

_____

_____

_____

Do you respect the other person's spiritual background or lack of?

___ Yes   ___ No   ___ Maybe   ___ Don't Know

If not, why?_____

_____

_____

_____

If you have the same spiritual background, what have they written, said or done that made you believe they are telling the truth?

_____

_____

_____

_____

Do the two of you share the same political views?

___ Yes   ___ No   ___ Maybe   ___ Don't Know

If not, does the other person respect your political viewpoints or lack of?

___ Yes   ___ No   ___ Maybe   ___ Don't Know

Do you respect the other person's political viewpoints or lack of?

___ Yes ___ No ___ Maybe ___ Don't Know

If not, why? _____

_____

_____

_____

Does the other person respect your choice for a career or a job?

___ Yes ___ No ___ Maybe ___ Don't Know

If not, why? _____

_____

_____

_____

Do you respect the other person's choice for a career or a job?

___ Yes ___ No ___ Maybe ___ Don't Know

Why or why not, or what do you need to find out to make a choice about their career?

_____

_____

_____

_____

If you are going to go to college, does the other person emotionally support or encourage you with your educational goals?

___ Yes ___ No ___ Maybe ___ Don't Know

If the other person is going to college, are you emotionally supporting or encouraging the other person's educational goals?

___ Yes ___ No ___ Maybe ___ Don't Know

Why or why not?_____

_____

_____

_____

Is the other person afraid for your health and/or safety?

___ Yes ___ No ___ Sometimes
___ Maybe ___ Don't Know

If so, what exactly is the other person scared about and why?

_____

_____

_____

_____

Are you afraid for the other person's health and/or safety?

___ Yes ___ No ___ Sometimes
___ Maybe ___ Don't Know

If so, why are you concerned about the other person's health and/or safety?

_____

_____

_____

_____

Internet Safety

Regarding the internet, be very careful when you write to people you've *never* met *in person*! Protect your personal information. The reason is, anyone can send a fake picture. They can be a criminal who says they are a priest and they may be a truthful person, but the problem is, *you just don't know*. It's better to stay safe instead of taking a risk by possibly putting yourself in danger!

Bad things happened in 2006 with myspace.com. Myspace.com was supposed to be for teenagers *only*. Some criminally minded adults got into myspace.com to find teenagers for evil purposes.

It's your choice who you choose to talk to on the internet. Think **_carefully_** about dating someone you meet over the internet! ***Create and set internet boundaries for meeting anyone you met over the internet.*** Your boundaries for people you date on the internet *should be stricter* than for people you meet in person.

(I suggest that you *don't date anyone you meet on the internet*. If you were my kid or close friend, I'd discourage you from dating anyone you meet over the internet.)

How long would you want to be writing back and forth over the internet before you feel safe talking to this person on the phone?

_____

_____

_____

What is everything *you* need or want to know about this person *before* talking to them on the phone?

_____

_____

_____

_____

How long would you want to talk to them on the phone *before* meeting them face-to-face?

___ Weeks ___ Months ___ Years

What is everything you need and want to know about this person over the phone before meeting them face-to-face?

_____

_____

_____

_____

Learning How to Manage Your Money

Do you want to manage your own money?

    ___ Yes   ___ No   ___ Don't Know

Why or why not?_____

_____

_____

_____

Do you want to learn how to manage your money?

    ___ Yes   ___ No   ___ Maybe   ___ Don't Know

Do you need to learn how to manage your money?

    ___ Yes   ___ No   ___ Maybe   ___ Don't Know

If you need or want to learn to budget your money, check all the people or agencies that you would trust to teach you money management skills:

    ___ Family
    ___ Friends
    ___ Your religious organization(s)
    ___ Social service organization/Non-profit organization
    ___ Others

What are the names of those people or organization(s)?

_____

_____

_____

A representative protective payee is only allowed to manage a person's government money. If you have an inheritance, life insurance, wages, or any other money coming in, a representative protective payee is not allowed to manage those. A trustee can handle all types of money no matter where it comes from. It can include stocks, bonds or insurance payments also.

Do you have a trustee?

___ Yes ___ No ___ Don't Know

If you want to know about stocks, bonds or trusts, ask your family, trustee, social service or financial agencies, or substitute decision maker.

Do you want a protective payee?

___ Yes ___ No ___ Maybe ___ Don't Know

Why or why not?_____

_____

_____

Who do you want your payee to be? (A protective payee usually works for many customers.)

_____

_____

This next section of three sets of questions has to do with what your beliefs are as far as giving money.

Do you believe in giving money to religious organizations?

___ Yes ___ No ___ Sometimes ___ Maybe
___ Not Sure ___ Don't Know

Why or why not?_____

_____

_____

_____

How much money a week, a month, a year, or every pay period would you want to give to a religious organization? (This could change as the amount of your income changes.)

_____

_____

Do you believe in giving money to non-profit organizations?

___ Yes ___ No ___ Sometimes
___ Maybe ___ Don't Know

If so, who?_____

_____

_____

How much money a week, a month, a year, or every pay period would you want to give to a non-profit organization? (This may change as the amount of your income changes.)

_____

_____

Do you believe in giving money to political candidates or political causes?

___ Yes ___ No ___ Sometimes
___ Maybe ___ Don't Know

Why or why not?_____

_____

_____

_____

How much money a week, a month, a year, or every pay period would you consider giving to a candidate or a cause? (This may change as the amount of your income changes.)

_____

_____

These next questions are to help you to know some of your boundaries, to know when others are financially hurting you and what your financial choices are!

What religious/spiritual causes would you consider giving part of your money to?

_____

_____

_____

What non-profit organizations would you consider giving part of your money to?

_____

_____

_____

What political causes would you consider giving part of your money to?

_____

_____

_____

These next questions ask what business you want to hold your money and what types of accounts you want to have.

Do you want to have your money in a credit union, a bank, or both?

___ Credit Union ___ Bank ___ Both ___ Don't Know

Which one and why?_____

_____

_____

Do you want a savings or checking account or both?

___ Savings ___ Checking ___ Both ___ Don't Know

Why?_____

_____

_____

How do you want to pay your bills? Do you want to pay by: (Check all ways that are acceptable to you.)

___ Money order
___ Checking account
___ Pay your bills online
___ Automatic bill payment
___ Debit Card

Why do you want to pay your bills that way?

_____

_____

_____

_____

Do you want to carry cash on hand?

___ Yes ___ No ___ Sometimes
___ Maybe ___ Don't Know

Why or why not?_____

_____

_____

_____

Do you know what a credit card is?

___ Yes ___ No ___ Don't Know

What is it? _____

_____

_____

_____

Do you want a credit card(s)?

___ Yes ___ No ___ Maybe ___ Don't Know

If so, how many?_____

Why would you want that many credit cards?

_____

_____

_____

Do you know what a debit card is?

    ___ Yes   ___ No   ___ Don't Know

Explain it. _____

_____

_____

Do you want a debit card(s)?

    ___ Yes   ___ No   ___ Maybe   ___ Don't Know

If so, how many? _____

Why would you want that many debit cards?

_____

_____

_____

General Money Safety

Would you feel safe if someone asked you, "How much money do you make?"

___ Yes ___ No ___ Maybe ___ Don't Know

Why or why not?_____

_____

_____

Do you think another employee would feel comfortable if you asked them, "How much money do you make?"

___ Yes ___ No ___ Maybe ___ Don't Know

Why or why not? _____

_____

_____

_____

Would you feel comfortable telling your friends how much money you make?

___ Yes ___ No

Why or why not?_____

_____

_____

_____

Is it smart to lend money to others?

    ___ Yes   ___ No   ___ Depends on the Situation
    ___ Depends on Who It Is   ___ Don't Know

If it depends on the situation, what would *your* guidelines be for lending money and who would *you* feel safe lending your money to?

_____

_____

_____

_____

Would you ever consider asking for money from others or does it depend on the situation?

    ___ Yes   ___ No   ___ Depends on the Situation
    ___ Don't Know

Why or why not, or under what circumstances would you say it's okay to ask someone for money?

_____

_____

_____

_____

Financial Safety

Who would you give your bank account number to?

_____

_____

Why would you give your bank account number to those people?

_____

_____

_____

Who would you give your Social Security number to?

_____

_____

Why would you give your Social Security number to those people?

_____

_____

_____

Who are the people you would give your bank account and Social Security information to?

_____

_____

Why would you give your bank account number and your Social Security number to those people?

_____

_____

_____

Would you want to talk to your support team *before* giving personal information to important people?

___ Yes ___ No ___ Maybe ___ Don't Know

Why or why not?_____

_____

_____

Who are the people your support team says can have your bank account and/or Social Security numbers?

_____

_____

Addictions

People who drink alcohol or smoke usually socialize, date, or marry people who drink or smoke; however, nonsmokers usually won't allow smoking in their home or car. Knowing why you **do** or **don't** smoke or drink will help you stick to your boundaries.

For example, as a nonsmoker, this one person talks to recovering alcoholics *on the phone* as long as they do not start drinking again. She will get together with them in public, but her smoking friends don't smoke in her home, and she usually doesn't go to their home. She will visit with smokers outside while they are smoking. She has her own reasons for associating with recovering friends and smoking friends from a distance!

Once you find out that something is "unsafe," "dangerous," or "unhealthy," think about avoiding those things. For example, if anyone in your professional or personal support team tells you that smoking, drinking, taking illegal drugs, or gambling are unhealthy, unsafe, dangerous, or risky, *think about* avoiding people who practice risky behaviors. If you need or want to find out why they are saying it is safe or unsafe, etc., it is reasonable to ask. Remember, you chose the people you want to help you when you don't know what questions to ask or choices to make.

If you choose to make a different choice than your support team, tell them why and what your protection barriers are.

Do your own research and talk it over with several trusted people.

Alcohol

Before making any choices about drinking alcohol, get information from all the resources you can find! You can call the Prevention Center at (509) 922-8383.

Talk to all your doctors and your pharmacy who know your personal medical and mental health history! It is your choice if you take someone with you or go alone.

As a woman, consider if you want to get pregnant in the future. (These next questions are for you to ask your doctor.)

Will alcohol have any negative effects on a child if you get pregnant?

___ Yes ___ No ___ Maybe ___ Don't Know
___ Does Not Apply

If the answer is yes or maybe, ask your doctor what the possible negative effects could be.

_____

_____

_____

Will the baby outgrow any of those negative effects?

_____

If you drink while pregnant, your baby could have developmental disabilities, mental health problems or physical disabilities! The more a woman drinks and/or takes illegal and prescription drugs while she is pregnant, the higher the risk that the child could be born with severe disabilities! I personally know ten adults with severe disabilities who must have someone around them, 24 hours a day, seven days a week!

Before choosing to drink, ask yourself the following questions:

Do you take prescription medicine?

___ Yes ___ No

Are you afraid of how drinking will make you feel?

___ Yes ___ No

What do you think about the health reasons? (I've heard there are benefits and risks.)

_____

_____

_____

Is the price of alcohol worth it?

___ Yes ___ No

Is the risk of addiction worth it to start drinking?

___ Yes ___ No

Do your religious beliefs agree or disagree with drinking?

___ Agree ___ Disagree

What do you know about people who committed crimes while they were drunk?

_____

_____

_____

Have you had any family members or friends killed by a drunk driver?

    ___ Yes   ___ No

Do you know any alcoholics?

    ___ Yes   ___ No

Do you know what a "recovering alcoholic" is?

    ___ Yes   ___ No

Do you know any recovering alcoholic?

    ___ Yes   ___ No

If after going through this list, you choose to drink, here are a few more questions for safety!

How are you going to protect yourself from getting addicted?

_____

_____

_____

How are you going to stay safe and not fall into the wrong crowd?

_____

_____

_____

If you can and want to drive, how will you keep yourself from driving drunk?

_____

_____

_____

Would you give your car keys to someone if you wanted to drink at a party?

___ Yes ___ No ___ Sometimes ___ Don't Know

Who could you give your car keys to if you want to drink at a party?

_____

Who would you give your car keys to?

_____

Who do you need and want to talk to about making the choice of who you would feel safe giving your car keys to temporarily until you are sober?

_____

How will you stop yourself from getting into a car with someone who has been drinking?

_____

_____

_____

Do you still want to drink alcohol?

___ Yes ___ No ___ Sometimes ___ Don't Know

Why or why not?_____

_____

_____

If you choose to drink, what are the health and safety barriers you would put in place (i.e., giving car keys to a friend until you sober up)?

_____

_____

_____

If you choose not to drink, why?

_____

_____

_____

If sometimes, in what situations is it okay to drink and in what situations is it not okay to drink?

_____

_____

_____

Smoking

Are you a smoker?

   ___ Yes __ No

Do you enjoy smoking?

   ___ Yes ___ No ___ Sometimes
   ___ Never Thought About It

Why or why not?_____

_____

_____

If you smoke, do you want to quit?

   ___ Yes ___ No ___ Sometimes
   ___ Maybe ___ Don't Know

Why or why not?_____

_____

_____

If you are currently a smoker, have you tried to quit smoking, and started smoking again?

   ___ Yes ___ No

If you are a smoker and want to continue smoking, I would encourage you to vape because vaping is not dangerous to others. If you choose to vape, I would strongly recommend you shop around and buy from a local store instead of buying online.

As a nonsmoker, I prefer being around those who vape because it smells better. Vaping does not affect secondhand smokers.

Two websites that speak of vaping are:

http://www.ecassoc.org
http://www.fda.gov

The people who work at the electronic cigarette association set standards. For a business to be part of the association, they must follow the standards of the association.

The people who work for the Food and Drug Administration test prescription drugs, over-the-counter drugs, and take complaints and compliments.

Have you researched vaping?

___ Yes ___ No

Have you decided that vaping is good or bad?

___ Good ___ Bad ___ Not Sure ___ Don't Know

Why?_____

_____

_____

Do you vape?

___ Yes ___ No

Why?_____

_____

_____

Will you start using electronic smoking devices?

___ Yes ___ No ___ Maybe ___ Don't Know

Why?_____

_____

_____

If you are a smoker, do you want to vape instead?

___ Yes ___ No ___ Maybe ___ Don't Know

Why?_____

_____

_____

Are you an ex-smoker (someone who used to smoke and no longer smokes)?

___ Yes ___ No

Are you a nonsmoker (someone who has never smoked in their life)?

___ Yes ___ No

Here are examples of closeness for the next few questions. If you are a smoker, answer the question regarding an ex-smoker or nonsmoker. If you are an ex-smoker or nonsmoker, answer the question regarding a smoker.

At what level do you feel comfortable being friends with a smoker, ex-smoker or nonsmoker?

___ Telephone friends
___ Friends that meet in neutral places like a restaurant, mall, school, or bus station
___ Online friends/Internet friends
___ Friends that visit at each other's houses

Why do you feel that way?

_____

_____

_____

_____

If you are a nonsmoker or ex-smoker, would you consider marrying a smoker?

___ Yes   ___ No   ___ Maybe   ___ Don't Know

Why or why not?_____

_____

_____

_____

How physically close to a smoker would you feel comfortable?

_____

_____

_____

Why or why not?_____

_____

_____

_____

Local Transportation

You can choose more than one way to travel around town!

Would you want to walk?

___ Yes ___ No ___ Sometimes
___ Maybe ___ Don't Know

If yes, how far?

____ Miles
____ Blocks

Where would you walk to?

_____

_____

_____

If no or don't know, why would you not want to walk to places?

_____

_____

_____

Would you consider riding a bike?

___ Yes ___ No ___ Sometimes
___ Maybe ___ Don't Know

If yes, how far?

____ Miles
____ Blocks

Where would you bicycle to?

_____

_____

_____

If no, maybe, or don't know, why?

_____

_____

_____

Are there any other forms of transportation you are willing to use?

___ Yes   ___ No   ___ Maybe   ___ Don't Know

If yes, what are they?

_____

_____

_____

If no, maybe, or don't know, who are the people you can talk to, to find out if there are acceptable ways to travel around?

_____

_____

_____

Disability Van
(Also Called Paratransit or Dial-a-Ride)

The disability van is a service offered to people who have severe enough disabilities that riding the city bus is too dangerous or difficult. You must apply and be **eligible** to ride the disability van. It is a door-to-door service. Passengers must schedule their rides in advance.

The county that you live in will determine how far in advance you must schedule your ride. (For example, Spokane County requires 2-7 days advance notice.)

Do you want to apply to ride the disability van?

___ Yes ___ No ___ Maybe ___ Don't Know

Why or why not?_____

_____

_____

_____

When do you need to ride? Here is a list. (Check all that apply for the disability van.)

___ Day
___ Night
___ Fall
___ Winter
___ Spring
___ Summer
___ Weekends
___ Go to unfamiliar areas
___ During the holidays that public transportation observes

Do you need a personal care attendant?

   ___ Yes   ___ No   ___ Sometimes   ___ Don't Know

City Bus

Riding the city bus involves being around everyone! People with no disabilities may ride the city bus for many different reasons. These reasons may include it costs too much money for gas to drive a lot, car insurance or the money to fix a broken down car, or people may just want to keep our air clean so they find other ways to get around town.

The city bus is quicker than the disability van in getting you where you want to go. It is not a door-to-door service.

Are you interested in riding the city buses?

____ Yes ____ No ____ Maybe ____ Don't Know

Why or why not?_____

_____

_____

Are you interested in learning *how* to ride the city buses?

____ Yes ____ No ____ Maybe ____ Don't Know

Why or why not?_____

_____

_____

If yes, who are all the people that you want to teach you?

_____

_____

If no, please share what you know about riding the city bus.

_____

_____

_____

If maybe or don't know, what do you need to find out to make an informed choice?

_____

_____

_____

Do you know any "safety tips" when riding the city bus?

    ___ Yes   ___ No

If yes, what are *your safety tips* that you use to keep yourself safe on the city bus?

_____

_____

_____

_____

Do you need help in knowing how to keep yourself safe when riding the city bus?

    ___ Yes   ___ No

If yes, who do you want to teach you safety tips for riding the city bus?

_____

_____

Driving

The most independent way to get around is by driving, but it is also the *most expensive* way to travel. Some people don't drive due to disability or because they broke the law.

Do you want to drive?

    ___ Yes   ___ No   ___ Not Sure

If you're not sure, what do you need to find out so you can make an informed choice?

_____

_____

_____

If yes, how much money do you need to save to buy a car?

    $ _____

How much money would you be willing to spend on a car?

    $ _____

How much money can you afford to budget every paycheck for gas, car insurance, and money for when your car needs to be repaired?

    $ _____

Some people like to carpool. "Carpool" means more than one person riding in a vehicle to the same place. This takes less gas money per person and gets more people to where they want to go.

Would you consider carpooling?

    ___ Yes ___ No ___ Sometimes
    ___ Maybe ___ Don't Know

Who would you carpool with? (Examples of this would be riding with smokers, religious people, co-workers, or only with people you know.)

_____

_____

_____

At what age do you think you will have enough maturity to drive?

_____ Years Old

What protection barriers would you want to be put in place to be a safe driver? (An example, who will you give your keys to *before* you start drinking alcohol, if you choose to drink alcohol?)

_____

_____

_____

_____

If you drink alcohol, how do you plan to get home?

___ Taxicab
___ Bus
___ Van
___ Family
___ Friend
___ Other

Do you know what driving accommodations are?

___ Yes ___ No

If yes, what are they?

_____

_____

_____

(Accommodations need to be specific to an individual's disability.)

Do you need any driving accommodations?

___ Yes ___ No ___ Maybe ___ Don't Know

If yes, what accommodations did you or your support team find that you need for driving (i.e., a steering ball, etc.)?

_____

_____

_____

If you don't know, ask your support team what driving accommodations are.

Employment

What was your dream job as a child?

_____

_____

_____

What was your dream job as a teenager?

_____

_____

_____

As a teenager, did you have a job?

____ Yes ____ No

If yes, how many?_____

If yes, where did you work? _____

_____

As an adult, how many hours do you think you can comfortably work a day?

_____ Hours

As an adult, how many dollars are you willing to accept as your lowest amount of pay per hour?

$_____

Would you *enjoy* a job?

____ Yes ____ No

Do you enjoy working on or with machines?

___ Yes ___ No

If yes, what kind of machines?

_____

_____

_____

Do you enjoy doing physical labor?

___ Yes ___ No

If yes, what kind of physical labor?

_____

_____

_____

Do you enjoy doing office work such as answering phones, typing on the computer, filing, and more?

___ Yes ___ No

If yes, how many words can you type a minute? _____

Do you enjoy doing data entry and working with different computer programs?

___ Yes ___ No

Do you enjoy fixing computers when they break?

___ Yes ___ No

Do you enjoy doing restaurant work which includes host/hostess, waiter/waitress, dishwasher, or cook?

___ Yes ___ No

Do you enjoy planting seeds or picking plants?

___ Yes ___ No

If yes, what kind of plants?

_____

_____

_____

Do you enjoy making clothes?

___ Yes ___ No

If yes, what kind of clothes?

_____

_____

_____

Do you enjoy engineering?

___ Yes ___ No

If yes, what kind of engineering?

_____

_____

_____

Do you enjoy aeronautics?

   ___ Yes ___ No

If yes, what kind of aeronautics?

_____

_____

_____

Do you enjoy working with the public?

   ___ Yes ___ No

Do you enjoy working with co-workers?

   ___ Yes ___ No

Do you enjoy working with other people?

   ___ Yes ___ No

Do you enjoy working alone?

   ___ Yes ___ No

This next set of questions is related to what **you are good at doing**! *Nobody is good at everything!*

Are you good at working with machines?

   ___ Yes ___ No

What kind of machines?

_____

_____

_____

Are you good at doing physical labor?

___ Yes ___ No

What kind of physical labor?

_____

_____

_____

Are you good at doing office work such as answering phones, typing on the computer, filing, and more?

___ Yes ___ No

Are you good at doing data entry and working with different computer programs?

___ Yes ___ No

Are you good at fixing computers when they break?

___ Yes ___ No

Are you good at restaurant work which includes host/hostess, waiter/waitress, a dishwasher, or a cook?

___ Yes ___ No

Are you good at planting seeds or picking plants?

___ Yes ___ No

Are you good at making clothes?

___ Yes ___ No

Are you good at engineering?

___ Yes ___ No

Are you good at aeronautics?

___ Yes ___ No

Are you good at working with the public?

___ Yes ___ No

Are you good at working with co-workers?

___ Yes ___ No

Are you good at working by yourself when other people are around you?

___ Yes ___ No

Are you good at working alone when no one is around?

___ Yes ___ No ___ Sometimes
___ Kind Of ___ Don't Know

How to Narrow Down Your Choice of Jobs

1) You can begin to narrow your choices by eliminating jobs that you don't enjoy and that you are not good at.
2) It would be smart to research jobs that you enjoy and that you are good at.
3) The next step would be to find the right amount of pay you are willing to accept.
4) Do you want a job that offers pay raises in the future?
5) Does the job you want to do require more education? If so, see the chapter on college.

Some jobs, like singing in a band, don't pay a lot of money but *might be* worth it. Another type of job that doesn't pay a lot are jobs at religious organizations. However, the spiritual rewards might be worth it!

Agencies that can help people find work:

- Developmental Disabilities Administration (DDA)
- Department of Vocational Rehabilitation (DVR)
- Services for the Blind

Is your best way of learning "On the Job Training?"

___ Yes ___ No ___ Depends on What the Job Is
___ Sometimes ___ Don't Know

If it depends on what the job is or you don't know, what would you need to find out to make an informed choice?

_____

_____

_____

Are there any agencies that will help you find a job that you enjoy doing?

____ Yes ____ No

What are the names of the agencies that could help you get the job of your dreams?

_____

_____

_____

If you are interested in earning a lot of money, a smart idea would be to consider going to college!

College

You have a better chance of getting a higher paying job if you go to college! The higher the college degree, the better paying job you should be able to get.

There are jobs you can get that you do not have to go to college for. However, if you go to college to get more skills, you have a better chance of getting a raise or a promotion at work! Some employers will not hire you unless you have a college degree.

In thinking about going to college, ask yourself these questions:

How much money do you need to make a month at a future job?

$_____

How much money do you want to make a month at a future job?

$_____

(When researching jobs, the pay may be presented as "$40K w/ med." This translates into earning $40,000 a year plus medical benefit. They assume you understand that any dollar amount they give means yearly amounts, not by the month, week, day, or hour unless specified.)

For all jobs you would enjoy and/or be good at, research them to find out if going to college is required for the job.

If going to college is required for some of these jobs, what are the required classes?

_____

_____

_____

What kind of degree do you need?

___ Less than 2 years ___ 2 year (AA) ___ 4 year (BA)
___ 6 year (MA) ___ 8 year (PhD) ___ Longer

In what area of study are you getting your college degree (for example, business, social work, medical, etc.)?

_____

_____

_____

Are you going to college to get a job?

___ Yes ___ No

If yes, there are grants, scholarships, loans, and work study programs specific to paying for college. If you have a disability, DVR, DDA, or Services for the Blind _might be_ able to help you find money to pay for college or will pay for your classes if you show them that you are serious about going to work.

If you are not going to college for employment reasons, look at different ways for college to be paid for, such as family, other scholarships, or government programs.

How are you going to pay for college?

_____

_____

_____

Do you want to go to college?

___ Yes ___ No ___ Maybe ___ Don't Know

If yes, for what degree and for how long? If no, maybe or don't know, what are your plans for work?

_____

_____

_____

_____

Wants

Choosing a Cell Phone Company

Strong recommendation: Take someone from your support team with you to a cell phone store. **Don't sign** any papers without someone you trust reading the paperwork and saying, "It is **safe to sign!**"

Cell phone words and definitions:

"Contract" means a legal document signed by everyone involved.

"Anytime minutes" means you pay a set amount of money each month for that number of minutes for specific hours of the day, and certain days of the week. Every cell phone company is different regarding anytime minutes and the days of the week. For example, anytime minutes could be 7:00 a.m. – 7:00 p.m. or it could be 9:00 a.m. – 9:00 p.m. **Ask the salesperson!**

"Text messaging" means sending a written message from one phone to another phone.

"Monthly plan" means how much you pay each month for the service of your choice.

"Dropped call" means a cell phone call ends before the conversation is complete. The cell phone company *should* reimburse you by giving you some free minutes or taking money off your bill or by giving you a credit on your bill. (Each cell phone company is different in the way they reimburse their customers!)

"Credit" means the cell phone company will deduct an amount from your bill. For example, if your bill was $100 and the cell phone company gave you a $20 credit, your bill would then be $80.

"Kickbacks" means the way cell phone companies (and other businesses) reward their customers for recommending their company to new customers.

Research all cell phone companies to see which one meets your needs and meets your price range!

Do you want a cell phone?

___ Yes ___ No ___ Maybe ___ Don't Know

Why or why not?_____

_____

_____

Do you think that you need a cell phone?

___ Yes ___ No ___ Maybe ___ Don't Know

Why or why not?_____

_____

_____

Cell Phone Prices

Would you give up something (i.e., cable) to pay for a cell phone?

___ Yes ___ No ___ Maybe ___ Don't Know

How would you pay your cell phone bill every month?

_____

_____

_____

Most or all cell phone companies require you to have a credit card or debit card to pay your bill over the phone or over the internet. If you would rather pay with check or money order, ask the company if that's okay.

Sometimes cell phone companies change the plans they offer. You need to be on a plan until your contract is over. When the contract is over, it's up to the cell phone company to ask you about keeping or changing your plan, or they might automatically update your plan to another plan with or without your permission. The updated plan will probably cost more and would probably be close to your current plan!

Some people choose to have a work cell phone and a personal cell phone. If you have two cell phones, you will need a contract for each phone number.

What is your most comfortable way of communicating with a cell phone company?

_____

_____

_____

Do you need/want to talk to a live customer service representative on the telephone?

___ Yes ___ No ___ Maybe ___ Don't Know

Do you need/want to use an automated telephone system?

___ Yes ___ No ___ Maybe ___ Don't Know

Do you have a computer?

___ Yes ___ No

If so, do you know how to use the internet to pay bills?

___ Yes ___ No

If so, would you consider paying your bills online?

___ Yes ___ No ___ Maybe ___ Not Sure
___ Don't Know

Why or why not?_____

_____

_____

If you answered yes to all three questions, would you feel safe doing your business on the internet?

___ Yes ___ No ___ Maybe ___ Don't Know

Why or why not?_____

_____

_____

The type of business you could be doing with a cell phone company is adding or canceling something.

Do you have the time to go to the store?

___ Yes ___ No

If you want to go to the store, where are the cell phone stores closest to you?

_____

_____

_____

Your Job Might Limit Your Choices!

Do you have a job?

___ Yes   ___ No

Does your job require you to have a cell phone?

___ Yes   ___ No   ___ Sometimes   ___ Don't Know

Does your place of work buy cell phones for its employees?

___ Yes   ___ No   ___ Don't Know

If the employer buys and pays for the employee's cell phone, the employer gets to choose the cell phone company and the plan; not you, unless the employer says you can!

If you use your cell phone for work, will your boss pay for part of your cell phone bill?

___ Yes   ___ No

If not and you want a cell phone, will you ask your boss to give you a cell phone for work?

___ Yes   ___ No

If they will, how much will they pay a month?

_____% or $_____

If yes, do you get to choose your cell phone company?

___ Yes   ___ No   ___ Don't Know

If you don't know, how will you find out?

_____

_____

_____

How many hours are you home to use your landline phone?

_____ Hours

If you think you need a cell phone, do you also need a landline phone?

___ Yes ___ No

Why or why not?_____

_____

_____

What are your responsibilities to your family (children or other adults) that would cause you to need a cell phone? (For example, there's a couple that both have a cell phone on the same account because if the child's school calls and cannot get one parent on the phone, they can call the other parent.)

_____

_____

_____

What is your reason for getting a cell phone?

_____

_____

_____

Are there any cell phone companies that will accommodate your disability?

___ Yes ___ No ___ Don't Know

If you don't know, how will you find out?

_____

_____

_____

Do any of the cell phone companies offer people with disabilities financial discounts?

___ Yes ___ No ___ Don't Know

If you don't know, how will you find out?

_____

_____

_____

Do the cell phone companies require proof of disability to get the discount?

___ Yes ___ No ___ Don't Know

Do any of the cell phone companies offer specials for college students?

___ Yes ___ No ___ Don't Know

If you don't know, how will you find out?

_____

_____

_____

Do any of the cell phone companies offer military personnel specials?

___ Yes ___ No ___ Don't Know

If you don't know, how will you find out?

_____

_____

_____

How important do you think it is to get insurance on a cell phone? (Check your answer.)

___ Very Important
___ Somewhat Important
___ Not Important
___ Don't Know

(Ask people close to you the reason for having insurance on a cell phone if you don't know anything about insurance.)

The next set of questions specifies where you call or receive calls from. Think about where your family and friends are located in the world (especially if they get assigned to another country).

Do you need any international minutes on your plan?

___ Yes   ___ No   ___ Maybe   ___ Don't Know

A way to think of international minutes is how many people you know who live in another country such as China or do you have any family or friends in the military (especially that could end up going to war).

If yes, how many international minutes do you need each month?

_____ Minutes

Do you need national minutes on your plan? (National minutes means all over the USA.)

___ Yes ___ No ___ Maybe ___ Don't Know

If yes, how many national minutes do you need each month?

_____ Minutes

Do you need any regional minutes on your plan? (Regional depends on the state and city you are in and each cell phone company has different regional areas they cover.)

___ Yes ___ No ___ Maybe ___ Don't Know

If yes, how many regional minutes do you need each month?

_____ Minutes

Do you need any local minutes on your plan?

___ Yes ___ No ___ Maybe ___ Don't Know

If yes, how many local minutes do you need each month?

_____ Minutes

Something to think about: Do you really need a landline if you have a cell phone? How often are you home to make and receive your phone calls? How many hours are you home a day? How many phones do you want on your cell phone account?

Here are a few examples to help you decide:

- Example #1: Some families buy a lot of cell phones for the household. The phones go to the man, the woman, and all the older children in this household.
- Example #2: In another family, the husband and wife have cell phones, but the children do not.

Out of Town Traveling

Make a few copies of this traveling chapter. Each copy is for a different trip.

Why do you need to travel?

_____

_____

_____

Why do you want to travel?

_____

_____

_____

Where do you need to travel?

_____

_____

_____

Where do you want or need to travel? (List all places that you are thinking of traveling to.)

_____

_____

_____

List the positives about each place you need or want to travel to.

_____

_____

_____

List the negatives about each place you need or want to travel to.

_____

_____

_____

How many positives and how many negatives are there for each place?

_____

_____

_____

Where is the final place you have chosen to travel to? (Choose one place!)

_____

Be specific when answering your support team's questions!

What month(s) and day(s) are you available for traveling?

_____

_____

_____

What month, day, and year have you chosen to leave town?

_____

_____

_____

What month, day, and year are you coming back?

_____

_____

_____

Are you going to travel with other people?

___ Yes ___ No ___ Maybe ___ Don't Know

How many people are you traveling with? _____

Who are they?

_____

_____

_____

What are the positives of each person you are considering traveling with?

_____

_____

_____

_____

What are the negatives of each person you are considering traveling with?

_____

_____

_____

_____

How much money do you need to save for your trip?

$_____

How much do you have saved now?

$_____

How much money do you still need to save?

$_____

Do you want to get a credit card for traveling out of town?

___ Yes ___ No ___ Maybe ___ Don't Know

Why or why not or what do you need to find out?

_____

_____

_____

Do you know how to use traveler's checks?

___ Yes ___ No

Do you have extra money for "the fun stuff" such as postcards and other souvenirs?

___ Yes ___ No

How much "extra money" do you want to take with you total?

$_____

An emergency fund is money saved that you don't plan on spending unless you have to. For example, a man came to Washington State in the winter driving his own car. When he left to go back to California, he hit black ice and crashed his car. He called someone in Spokane, Washington to give him a ride and he had to use his emergency money to buy an airline ticket to fly home.

Do you have extra money to put in an emergency fund that you can take with you?

___ Yes ___ No

If you are a spiritual person and you will be traveling alone, talk to one close male and one close female friend who share your spiritual values so you can be held accountable to your spiritual values while you are away from the people you know.

If you are recovering from an addiction(s), you will need and want to be held accountable by talking to others recovering from the same addiction(s). Talk to one male and one female who are recovering from the same addiction(s) that you are. These people should be able to help you stick to your religious and/or recovery beliefs when you are traveling.

What is the crime rate in the city and state you are going to?

_____

_____

What kind of crime(s) happen most often in the city you are visiting?

_____

_____

Are the people friendly where you're going?

____ Yes   ____ No   ____ Don't Know

Do people in that town make eye contact? (For example: In the Pacific Northwest, most of the people are friendly, make eye contact, and help their neighbors. In general, in New York, if you make eye contact with someone, they will usually wonder what you want.)

____ Yes   ____ No   ____ Don't Know

When it comes to purchasing travel accommodations and transportation, shop around. If you have time, look for discount prices for traveling and hotel/motel. In restaurants, share the cost of meals by sharing a meal. Share a hotel/motel room together. Travel around the city together and share the cost of the taxicabs, rent-a-car, or the gas in somebody's personal vehicle. Share the cost of transportation to the city you are traveling to. For example, is there a buy two tickets for the price of one sale? If so, two people can pay half price for their ticket and both people can go!

How do you plan on getting to the city and state you are visiting? (Check the ONE that applies.)

____ Airplane
____ Greyhound Bus
____ Train
____ Driving Your Own Car

Other: _____

How are you paying to get there? (Check all that apply.)

____ Pay in Person
____ Pay over the Phone
____ Pay over the Internet

___ Pay with Cash
___ Pay with Travelers Check
___ Pay with Credit Card
___ Pay with Debit Card
___ Pay through PayPal
___ Pay with Check
___ Share Cost

How many people can you share the transportation cost with?

_____

How do you plan on traveling around the city you are visiting? (Check all that apply.)

___ Disability Van
___ City Bus
___ Driving your own car
___ Rent-a-car
___ Taxicab
Other: _____

How do you plan on paying for your transportation in the town you are in? (Check all that apply.)

___ Share the cost
___ Pay with Cash
___ Pay with Traveler's Check
___ Pay with Debit Card
___ Pay with Credit Card
___ Pay with Money Order
___ Pay with Check
___ Riding around with a friend/family member who lives in the town you are visiting

If you are going to share the cost, how many people are you going to share the cost with?_____

If it takes you a couple of days until you get there, where will you stay until you get there? Be specific with names of the hotel/motel and/or friends, the addresses, phone numbers, and email addresses.

_____

_____

_____

_____

Where will you be staying when you arrive in town? (Check all that apply.)

___ Hotel/Motel   ___ Family   ___ Friend

Will you be sharing the shelter cost with anyone?

___ Yes   ___ No   ___ Maybe   ___ Don't Know

How many people will be sharing the shelter cost? _____

How much money will your share of the shelter cost be per night?

$_____

If you stay in a hotel/motel, does your room have a kitchenette?

___ Yes   ___ No   ___ Maybe   ___ Don't Know

Are you going to buy groceries?

___ Yes   ___ No   ___ Maybe   ___ Don't Know

If your room has a kitchenette, are you going to cook food in the kitchenette?

___ Yes   ___ No   ___ Sometimes   ___ Maybe
___ Don't Know

Are you going to eat out at restaurants?

   ___ Yes ___ No ___ Sometimes ___ Maybe
 ___ Don't Know

How many of you will be sharing one plate of food?_____

When you split a large meal, will you be splitting the cost among all the people who eat that meal?

   ___ Yes ___ No ___ Sometimes ___ Maybe
 ___ Don't Know

Will you be eating at family members' or friends' houses?

   ___ Yes ___ No ___ Sometimes ___ Maybe
 ___ Don't Know

If eating at a family member's or friend's house, will you be helping them with the cost of the food?

   ___ Yes ___ No ___ Sometimes ___ Maybe
 ___ Don't Know

(Some family and friends will not accept money for food when you are staying in their home, others will.)

Is this a planned trip?

   ___ Yes ___ No

Is this an emergency trip? (Ex., family emergency)

   ___ Yes ___ No

If this is an emergency trip and you have a job, put in a "leave of absence."

If you don't or won't do financial business over the internet, consider asking for another person's help. For example, a man I know went to Kansas. He asked his sister to buy the ticket over the internet and to get a receipt. When she showed her brother the receipt, he paid his sister back. It was as if he had bought the ticket himself; but the price was cheaper over the internet than on the phone or in person. (His sister bought it at the cheapest rate.)

When flying, find someone to take you to the airport or take public transportation. If you park at the airport during your trip, you will be charged for *every hour* your car is parked there.

When planning your trip, list the things that need to be done and check things off as they get done:

____ Put a hold on the mail
____ Put a hold on the newspaper
____ Find someone to feed the pets
____ Find someone to water the plants
____ Find someone to stay at your house while you are on vacation (if you trust someone to stay in your home)!

Check to see if you have bought and packed all your necessities for your trip. Check your list twice, once for being bought and a second time for being packed.

Cross off each thing as it gets done:

____ Prescription medications
____ Personal Hygiene (hairbrush, toothbrush, toothpaste, mouthwash, floss)
____ Cell Phone or phone card
____ Cell Phone Charger
____ Traveler's Checks
____ Laptop Computer
____ Your ticket (bus, airplane, train, etc.)

Do you have a child or children going with you?

____ Yes ____ No

How many children? _____

Make a list of every child's needs and wants. As you put each thing in your suitcase for your children, cross it off the list so you know it's packed just like your stuff is packed.

It would be recommended when you are done packing to talk to someone on your support team to see if you have forgotten anything. Do this every time you take a trip.

Now, you are ready to go. You might want to make a second list for your return trip. (Things to buy and pack.)

Looking for a Close Relationship

(Make copies of this chapter. Use it for each significant relationship.)

What are your hobbies?

_____

_____

_____

What are the other person's hobbies?

_____

_____

_____

What hobbies do the two of you have in common?

_____

_____

_____

What hobbies do the two of you have that are different?

_____

_____

_____

Does the other person respect your hobbies?

    ___ Yes ___ No ___ Maybe ___ Don't Know

Do you respect the other person's hobbies?

    ___ Yes ___ No ___ Maybe ___ Don't Know

Why or why not?

_____

_____

_____

Can the other person accept all of your bad habits (such as biting your fingernails, smoking, or drinking alcohol)?

    ___ Yes ___ No ___ Maybe ___ Don't Know

Can you accept all of the other person's bad habits (such as biting your fingernails, smoking, or drinking alcohol)?

    ___ Yes ___ No ___ Maybe ___ Don't Know

How do you cope with their bad habits?

_____

_____

_____

How do they cope with your bad habits?

_____

_____

_____

How long would you want to know someone before you would feel comfortable being touched by the other person?

_____

What kind of touch? (Please specify the time)

    ___ Holding hands: How long? _____
    ___ Hugging: How long? _____
    ___ Kissing: How long? _____
    ___ Nuzzling nose to nose: How long? _____

How long would you need to know someone before you would "feel safe" giving a person your phone number?

    ___ Days   ___ Weeks   ___ Months   ___ Years

What would make you "feel safe" about giving a person your phone number?

_____

_____

_____

How long would you need to know someone before you would "feel safe" giving a person your email address?

    ___ Days   ___ Weeks   ___ Months   ___ Years

What would make you "feel safe" about giving that person your email address?

_____

_____

_____

How long would you need to know someone before you would "feel safe" giving someone (especially someone who has a crush on you) your physical address?

___ Days ___ Weeks ___ Months ___ Years

What would make you "feel safe" about giving that person your physical address?

_____

_____

_____

Do you have children?

___ Yes ___ No

Do you want to have children?

___ Yes ___ No

Why or why not?_____

_____

_____

Dating, living together, and marrying on the rebound are usually bad. "Rebound" means going into another relationship before your broken heart has had a chance to heal from the last relationship.

Raising Children

Do you ever want to have children?

    ___ Yes   ___ No   ___ Maybe   ___ Don't Know

Why or why not?_____

_____

_____

Have you ever taken care of an animal(s)?

    ___ Yes   ___ No

If so, what kind of animal(s)?

_____

_____

If not, why have you never taken care of any animal(s)?

_____

_____

_____

Do you have *younger* brothers or sisters?

    ___ Yes   ___ No

If you do, did you ever take care of them?

    ___ Yes   ___ No

Have you ever taken care of other younger relatives, such as nieces, nephews, or cousins?

    ___ Yes   ___ No

Have you ever taken any babysitting or childcare classes?

   ___ Yes   ___ No

Have you ever done childcare for the neighborhood or for a religious organization?

   ___ Yes   ___ No

Have you ever taken any parenting classes?

   ___ Yes   ___ No

How do you handle stress in your day-to-day life?

_____

_____

_____

How do you handle the stress of things changing every day?

_____

_____

_____

How do you think you would handle those same stressful situations with a child or children living with you?

_____

_____

_____

How do you *think* you would handle *changes* with a child as they grow and mature? (Changes could be the way a child needs to be disciplined as they get older.)

_____

_____

_____

Do you want to be a natural parent?

___ Yes ___ No ___ Maybe ___ Don't Know

Why or why not?_____

_____

_____

Do you want to be a stepparent? (A stepparent is someone who marries one of the child's parents but is not the natural parent of that child.)

___ Yes ___ No ___ Maybe ___ Don't Know

Why or why not?_____

_____

_____

Do you want to be part of a blended family? (A blended family is when both adults bring children into the family from a previous relationship/marriage.)

___ Yes ___ No ___ Maybe ___ Don't Know

Why or why not?_____

_____

_____

Do you want to live with someone who has children?

___ Yes ___ No ___ Maybe ___ Don't Know

Why or why not?_____

_____

_____

There are different kinds of children who are up for adoption. They are different by age, the country they were born in, the reason they are up for adoption, and the type of adoption. Depending on your family, cultural and ethnic background, adoption may or may not be a good idea.

There are open adoptions, closed adoptions, relative adoptions, private adoptions, public adoptions, state-to-state adoptions, and international adoptions.

"Open adoption" means allowing the child or children to stay in contact with their birth parents in some way.

"Closed adoption" means the child or children have no contact with the birth parents and/or may not even know who their birth parents are.

Do you want to adopt a child or children?

___ Yes ___ No ___ Maybe ___ Don't Know

Why or why not?_____

_____

_____

If yes, what age group are you looking at adopting?

_____

What gender are you looking at adopting?

    ___ Male   ___ Female

Do you want to adopt a child in the USA?

    ___ Yes   ___ No   ___ Doesn't Matter   ___ Don't Know

Do you want to adopt a child born outside the USA?

    ___ Yes   ___ No   ___ Doesn't Matter   ___ Don't Know

Is there a child in your extended family that some other adult in your family cannot take care of?

    ___ Yes   ___ No   ___ Don't Know

If there is a child in your extended family that the parents are unable to raise, would you want to adopt that child to keep them in the family?

    ___ Yes   ___ No   ___ Maybe   ___ Don't Know

Why or why not?_____

_____

_____

If "maybe" or "don't know," what do you need to find out to make an informed choice?

_____

_____

_____

Would you want to adopt if it was going to be an open adoption?

    ___ Yes   ___ No   ___ Maybe   ___ Don't Know

Why or why not?_____

_____

_____

Would you want to adopt if it was going to be a closed adoption?

___ Yes ___ No ___ Maybe ___ Don't Know

Why or why not?_____

_____

_____

Do you want to be a guardian of a child?

___ Yes ___ No ___ Maybe ___ Don't Know

You can be a foster parent without adopting! Foster parents take children in temporarily during the time the court says the parents can't take care of their children. Some of the children who don't have parents are waiting for someone to adopt them. It may be that parents refuse to deal with their kids who break the law or it may be their kids take too much care due to their disability.

Foster parents see children come and go all the time, sometimes even in the middle of the night and/or without letting them know ahead of time!

Foster parents are employed by the state they live in. Being a foster parent is a 24 hour a day, 7 day a week job. A foster parent is not allowed to get regular childcare. When the foster parent needs some time for themselves, the foster parent *must find* another licensed foster care family, with the same criteria that they have.

Do you want to be a foster parent?

___ Yes ___ No ___ Maybe ___ Don't Know

If yes, what kind of children? (Check all that apply.)

    ___ Children or teenagers who have broken the law.
    ___ Children or teenagers who are developmentally delayed.
    ___ Children or teenagers who are developmentally disabled.
    ___ Children or teenagers who have a mental illness.
    ___ Children or teenagers who are orphans.
    ___ Children or teenagers who have been abused.
    ___ Children or teenagers who have emotional and/or behavioral issues.
    ___ Children or teenagers who have chemical dependency problems.

What age? (Check all that apply.)

    ___ Infants
    ___ Toddlers
    ___ Preschoolers
    ___ Elementary children
    ___ Younger teenagers
    ___ Older teenagers

When it's time to find a childcare provider to take a break, how will you choose someone who is safe to watch your own child(ren)?

_____

_____

_____

How much do you need to pay the childcare provider?

    $____

Whose house will your child(ren) stay at? (Check answer.)

___ Child(ren)'s house ___ Sitter's house

How long will you be out?

_____

Do you have the money to pay *both* the childcare provider *and* to pay for your outing?

___ Yes ___ No

Resources for the Disability Community

There are many types of resources for the disability community.

Public transportation helps everyone go anywhere in town. Public transportation also helps people save money!

There are many kinds of assistant living homes to choose from. There are adult family homes, group homes, CCF's, care centers, and independent living centers to learn independent living skills.

Other resources can help people gain employment. Resources could be Developmental Disabilities Administration (DDA), Division of Vocational Rehabilitation (DVR), or Services for the Blind; however, there are others.

A credit card is another type of resource. It can be used if you need to buy something or put something on hold over the phone. However, one credit card is all you need! The reason is, the more credit cards a person has, the easier it is to go into debt. "Debt" means spending more money than you have.

Not only do you owe the money that you spent buying something using the credit card, you will also have to pay it back plus interest. (Ask another person what "interest" means.) Paying interest when you don't have to is bad for you financially!

When considering buying an expensive item, take someone from your support team with you to verify if the purchase is worth the price. There's a <u>lower chance</u> of being taken advantage of and <u>once you learn to price things correctly</u>, you won't need as much assistance. You may need to ask someone for help to get it home when you buy a large item. An example is if you buy a TV, it would be hard to take it home on the bus.

If a person has trouble managing money and they receive money from Social Security Administration, Social Security Administration might insist that you have "representative protective payee."

"Representative protective payee" is a phrase used only by Social Security Administration for a person who takes care of their client's money. The person who has the disability can usually choose who their representative payee is. However, Social Security Administration **must** approve of the representative protective payee that the person has chosen. *The representative protective payee can only manage government money!*

A trustee takes care of all other financial resources. (If you need help understanding the difference between a representative protective payee and a trustee, ask your support team.) A trustee takes care of a "trust." A "trust" can be for an education, extraordinary medical expenses, work accommodations, or other reasons.

Another type of resource is an assistive device. An example of an assistive device is a link/typing board to know what a person who is nonverbal is saying. Another kind of assistive device is grab bars that the State and/or Federal government requires businesses to have.

If you want to live alone but have problems taking care of your personal care tasks, COPES and Personal Care Medicaid are two resources to help you live alone. These programs help people with things they are unable to do for themselves.

The rules for these programs depend on the state you live in. (You *must have* a certain number of personal care tasks *to be eligible* for either service.)

Family and friends are resources. They can help with any transportation and housework you need if you don't have enough hours. The government might say you are eligible for less hours than you really need.

Do you want to see if your family or friends want or can assist you *sometimes*?

___ Yes   ___ No   ___ Maybe   ___ Don't Know

Don't take advantage of your family or your friends! (It's not considered "taking advantage" _when_ that person _is going to the same place you_ are or the same direction you are at the same time.)

Every state has a large resource directory to find all the resources you need in your area. The number to dial is 211.

There are resources for getting and maintaining the correct weight, managing money, assertiveness training, etc.

Assertiveness training will be your **best defense** against someone taking advantage of you because you'll have the skills you need to prevent someone from taking advantage of you and the skills to ask for what you need! If you learn to be assertive, life will be safer.

The last two resources are self-advocacy and group advocacy if you disagree with any decision about services, such as being denied services.

When everyone with disabilities are being denied for the same reason, it is time to go talk to the politicians and fight for everyone with disabilities and their rights! (This works for any group of people who are being treated disrespectfully or being denied something that other people get.)

"Self-advocacy" is an individual fighting to get something they are entitled to and need but have been denied! These would be services the law already has in place, but an individual person has been denied. It could also be an individual fighting to get rid of a service/benefit they need and are eligible for.

"Group advocacy" is a group of people fighting for their rights to be treated equal, to have the same rights everyone does. It could be fighting for things that lawmakers might think we don't need. So, as a group, they stand up together and tell the politicians what they need!

Here are some questions to ask yourself when you consider using resources for the disability community.

How do you travel around town?

    ___ Disability Van
    ___ City Bus
    ___ Personal Car
    ___ Bicycle
    ___ Walking

What is your choice of housing?

    ___ Assisted Living
    ___ Renting a Room
    ___ Living Alone
    ___ Living with Chosen Roommates

If you want to live alone, do you need help with personal care or managing your money?

    ___ Yes ___ No ___ Maybe
    ___ Sometimes ___ Don't Know

Do you need help to get a job or maintain your job?

    ___ Yes ___ No ___ Maybe
    ___ Sometimes ___ Don't Know

If so, what organization helps you?

_____

_____

_____

Do you want or need assistance with pricing expensive items?

    ___ Yes ___ No ___ Maybe
    ___ Sometimes ___ Don't Know

Can you be assertive in stating your opinions?

    ___ Yes ___ No ___ Maybe
    ___ Sometimes ___ Don't Know

Can you comfortably ask for what you need and want?

    ___ Yes   ___ No   ___ Maybe
    ___ Sometimes   ___ Don't Know

Do you know where to go if you are denied services you need to maintain your independence?

    ___ Yes   ___ No

If so, where will you go if you are denied services?

_____

_____

_____

If not, what do you need to do to find out where you can go if you are denied services?

_____

_____

_____

Who are your "natural supports"? (A "natural support" is anyone around you who helps you who is not getting paid to help you.)

_____

_____

_____

The Challenges of Living on Your Own

Here are some words and simple definitions:

Interests: Things people enjoy. Everyone's interests are different.

Hobbies: Things and activities people spend their energy, money, and time on. Hobbies can be done with someone else or by yourself.

Goals: Things you want to achieve or accomplish in the short and long term.

Support Groups: Places you go to when you want and need to stop addictions. The people in these groups make good community friends and phone friends. However, it might not be safe to give your physical address to people in addiction type support groups.

Other types of support groups: This kind of support group is where people share the same kind of disability. I would strongly recommend knowing a person for one year before giving them your physical address.

Support Team: *All* of your professional and personal support groups put together. This includes your power of attorney/guardian, close friends, people from your place of worship, family members you choose, advocates, political friends, and social service places.

If you want to move out on your own, here are some safety tips to think about!

A) Know yourself. Know your boundaries when looking to be a roommate or looking for a roommate. Know yourself well enough to know if you can live happily with the person you just met to be their roommate.

B) Know what your best way of communicating with others is.

C) Set your boundaries around your property, your home, time that people are allowed to call you, and when they are allowed to come to your house. Make sure possible roommates share your values and boundaries.

Don't try to be friends with everyone; you won't have enough time for yourself and you will probably burn out!

Plan your days by what you *have to do*. First, this would include going to your doctor appointments, school or work, and taking care of yourself and family (including children). Taking care of yourself might be going out on a date or out with your significant other. Taking care of your child(ren) is finding someone *you trust* to watch your child(ren) when you go out, who will keep your child(ren) healthy, have the child(ren) obey *your* rules, and help the child(ren) do their schoolwork.

You need to make time for calling people on the phone. These calls could be to the doctors, child's schoolteacher, disability van service, your support team, etc.

If you run short on time, it may be worth the financial investment to get a cell phone. If you drive, get an earpiece for your cell phone! A cell phone is also worth having for long distance calls or if you need to call for a ride. Using a phone while traveling as a passenger is considered "good time management!"

Things you can do as a passenger on a disability van, city bus, or as a passenger in a car include calling your friends, making doctor's appointments for the family, writing a grocery list, doing homework, or do work that you have to take home from work.

Other members of the household can contribute by working and paying bills or doing other things such as chores around the house. When everyone contributes, the family has time to be together!

These are everyday necessities:

- Take care of personal hygiene
- Take your medicines

- Eat at least 3 big meals a day, or 5-6 small ones a day, or any mix of big and small meals. (This will usually include cooking, at other times eating at someone's house, and other times eating out.)
- Take time to sleep

All your planning should be done in seven-day weekly periods of time.

Is Guardianship Good or Bad?

In the author's opinion, if a person with a disability is educated but keeps making the same mistake, a power of attorney/guardian should not be legally responsible for any mistakes made by the person. If the person with the disability is not informed, the power of attorney/guardian **should be** legally responsible for those mistakes. It is best for the power of attorney/guardian to advise them of **all** possible consequences. They should not interfere with their right to make mistakes unless they are at risk of hurting another person or definitely hurting themselves medically or suffering extreme financial hardship by signing a contract. In the author's opinion, you should handle your own money if you are willing to accept responsibility for good choices and all the bad choices you make! It's also the author's opinion that a person must prove responsible with money in order to be able to legally sign a contract! People without a guardian have the responsibility and the right to speak up for themselves! You have the right to *choose* who you want to make choices for you if/when the court says that you are incompetent/incapacitated.

Advocates, different kinds of powers of attorney, trustees, advanced directives, wills, or a living will are _all less restrictive options_ to keep your health protected.

(If you want or need to know what the above words mean, ask a lawyer or the most knowledgeable person on your support team.)

Do you want a medical advanced directive?

___ Yes ___ No ___ Maybe ___ Don't Know

Why or why not?_____

_____

_____

If you want one, do you need help to fill it out?

   ___ Yes   ___ No

If yes, who do you want to help you?

_____

Do you want a mental health advanced directive?

   ___ Yes ___ No ___ Maybe ___ Don't Know

Why or why not?_____

_____

_____

Take reasonable health precautions and take responsibility for your own actions!

The answer(s) are up to you; however, here are some terms and their definitions:

"Surrogate decision-maker" means someone who makes the choices for a protected person when someone is unable to make choices for himself/herself anymore. The choices a surrogate decision-maker make are the same as if you are able to make your own choices.

As I try to teach the readers what some of the words or phrases mean, I will take you through the legal process by using easier language, BUT CHECK WITH A LAWYER!

"Guardianship" is a legal process to see if someone needs a guardian. Guardianship falls under the judicial branch of the government. It is an excellent idea for a judge or jury to see and hear who they are making a choice about.

*THIS INFORMATION IS NOT TO BE USED IN PLACE OF A LAWYER! IF YOU NEED LEGAL ADVICE, TALK TO A LAWYER!

"Represent" means someone who stands up for another person.

Since *most* people *do not* like other people having control over their life, a judge or jury will try to find the least restrictive alternative.

"Least Restrictive Alternative" means looking at other choices such as having any kind of power of attorney, an advocate, a trustee, or a representative protective payee before considering giving someone as a guardian.

"Judge" means one person who chooses the results of a court case.

"Jury" is a group of people who chooses the results of a court case. To the best of my understanding, the guardianship process gets started when someone applies to be a guardian over a proposed protected person. They go to Superior Court at the County Courthouse where a guardian ad litem is assigned.

Here is what some of the words or phrases below mean:

"Proposed": When the word **proposed** is used **before** the words "guardian," "ward," "protected person," or "vulnerable person," it means the judge or jury is in the process of making a choice about the proposed ward. If the ruling comes back that a guardian is needed, the word "proposed" is dropped. If this person needs protection, then they are a ward of the State. They can also be called, "ward," "protected person," or "vulnerable person." If they don't need protection, they aren't called anything special. They are "free" to make their own choices!

"Guardian ad litem" (GAL) is a temporary guardian. Their job ends when a judge or jury makes a decision if the person needs a guardian and if a guardian needs to be limited or full. A GAL is usually a lawyer appointed by Superior Court. A GAL's job is to find out what is in the best interest of the proposed person. The guardian ad litem MUST get medical, mental health, behavioral, educational (IQ) records, and the person's preferences. The GAL **must** talk to everyone involved in the person's life **including the person** that the choice will affect. These people include the caregivers, the proposed guardian, close and extended family that have an interest in this person, and close friends which could include life-long neighbors, friends, clergy, etc. The *GAL must meet with the "person"* whose life will be affected.

When the GAL is finished with their interview, he/she must write a report to the judge or jury about what he/she feels would be **'the safest'** least restrictive choice if one is possible, before a guardian would be chosen. (Sources: Guardianship Services of Seattle and National Guardianship Association Inc.)

A GAL is a lawyer that does not need to have any human services skills to be hired. It should be part of a GAL's job description to meet with the proposed person, but it is not! A GAL might have human services skills, but human services skills are not required for the job, so it's rare to find a GAL who has human services skills. If anyone knows anything factual (including personality differences) between a proposed guardian and a proposed protected person, report it to the GAL.

"Interested person" means anyone in the public who has a valid concern for a proposed protected person. Interested people need to make their concerns known based on fact, not opinion!! (Make concerns known to the guardian ad litem.)

Having events, dates of specific joys or problems, and the results helps the GAL write the report to the court.

It would be very wise to go to the protected person's hearing if you have concerns and it would be the responsible thing to do especially if the GAL does not listen to you!

During the hearing, the judge or jury will make a decision of how competent or incompetent and how capacitated or incapacitated a proposed protected person is.

"Competence" means the ability to get something done and the person's ability to solve problems.

"Incompetence" means a person's lack of problem solving skills.

"Capacitated" means what a person can physically do.

"Incapacitated" means a person's lack of ability to do things physically because he/she can't move. This person might not be able to use their feet or their hands or both. In this case, a person may be very smart, like Christopher Reeves. (Christopher Reeves was as an actor, director, and advocate; but he couldn't move, therefore he was incapacitated.)

At the end of the guardianship hearing, the judge or jury chooses if the person needs a guardian. They also choose the most qualified person for the job if the person needs a guardian. The judge/jury might try to match the person's needs, wants and personality with a guardian; however, they're not required to and probably won't!

"Protected person": If a judge or jury says the person is incompetent and/or incapacitated the word "proposed" is dropped. After the guardianship hearing, this person becomes a "**protected person**."

"Limited guardian" is a guardian who has the final say on specific areas of a protected person's life and those areas are written down. There are many kinds of limited guardians. The most common are guardian of the person and guardian of the estate.

"Guardian of the person" has power over the person such as their medical and health life and possibly anything that requires a "signature." (I don't know if a "guardian of the person" has any other jobs.)

"Signature" means signing your name.

A lawyer (including a free lawyer) can help you, the person, know what you can legally do and what you cannot legally do and what has become the guardian's job!

"Guardian of the estate" has control over large amounts of money such as a protected person's house, vehicle, property, stocks, bonds, and mutual funds, etc. A guardian of the estate has more power than a representative protective payee; however, they can do the same tasks as a representative protective payee.

"Bond" means a kind of insurance that protects the person's assets and money.

"Assets" are things that are expensive or of high value, but that is *not* cash, check, credit card or debit card. An asset could be stocks, bonds, owning a home, or a car. It could also be real gold, or real silver, or anything else antique.

"Full guardian" has 100% responsibility for the protected person even if that includes the requirement of talking to the protected person and getting their opinion. They don't always have to get their opinion before making a choice.

What happens if the guardian needs or wants to go on a vacation, gets sick, or is temporarily incompetent, or temporarily incapacitated, or dies? The standby guardian temporarily fills in until the regular guardian is back in town, is no longer sick or someone applies to be the new guardian if the original guardian becomes permanently incompetent, temporarily incapacitated, or dies.

Anyone can apply to be a guardian, but the judge or jury will usually consider a family member first and after the first guardian and standby guardian have been assigned, the next in line to be considered a guardian would be the standby guardian. I'm guessing because they already have access to the person's records and can make the quickest decision that is safe and healthy for someone even if it's not the protected person's choice.

"Standby guardian" is the guardian who legally substitutes for the guardian when the guardian is unavailable!

A guardian is NEVER allowed to make choices based on their own needs, wants, values, beliefs, goals, etc. The protected person is their OWN INDIVIDUAL SELF with their OWN needs, wants, values, beliefs, goals, etc. If the guardian does makes choices for their protected person based on the guardian's own values, that is *illegal* and *wrong*!

Any concerned person can apply to be someone's guardian! The job requirements of being a guardian or a standby guardian is they must be 18 years old or older, living in the same State as the protected person, have a sound mind, and *must never* have been convicted of a felony.

On a legislative level, guardians have been given two guidelines in the process of decision-making. They are 'substitute judgment' and 'best interest.'

"Substitute judgment" occurs when a guardian finds out *how* the protected person made choices *before* they became incapacitated. The guardian must look at the person's *overall lifestyle* including their social, religious, political, multicultural, and economic lifestyle—*everything that is important to the person*!

"The principle of substituted judgment is considered to be the manner in which the autonomy, values, beliefs, and preferences, of the protected person are best protected." (Source: National Guardianship Inc. www.guardianship.org)

The *only* concerns that could override the protected person's desires would be *health* and *safety* issues.

"A person's history" means everything that's happened from birth to now!

On the other hand, if a guardian cannot find anything out about a protected person's likes and dislikes, wants, desires, or how they would make their choices, the second guideline for making choices for a protected person is their 'best interest.'

"Best interest" means safety and health.

The author's only understanding of 'guardianship' is substitute judgment/substitute decision-maker for the person's *health*. It is an excellent idea for the guardian to listen to the concerns and wishes of the protected person if there's time before making medical choices on their behalf.

In order for a guardian to make the choice that would be closest to the protected person's personal choice, the guardian must learn as much as possible about the person they are protecting. The exception is making choices in the case of a medical emergency.

Best interest includes health and safety, and when the protected person has NO personal history of making choices, the guardian needs to see what a competent person's choice would be, given the same situation or circumstances. Safety and health are most American citizens two most important issues.

"Guardians may have to get advice from medical, financial and special ethics committees" in order to act in the best interest of the protected person.

I saw a situation where a woman could speak, had no power of attorney or guardian, and was talking to her doctor, mental health provider, and had a care giving agency, and caseworker **who were not listening to her and they were not working together in her best interests**!

If she had had a Spring Power of Attorney, this person would have taken control until she could speak for herself, but she would have needed to have the paperwork completed before the crisis!

Even if she had a guardian for medical reasons only, all the doctors would have been legally answerable to the power of attorney or guardian instead of answering to the lady who was falling apart medically at the time. She finally died because no one would listen to her, including the caregivers who came to help a couple of hours a day, a couple of days a week.

Guardians must work with all doctors with respect to a person's health issues and to a person's disabilities, including the need for special diets. I think a power of attorney has to work with a medical committee *unless a person has told the* power of attorney his/her wishes! (Check this information with a lawyer if you are interested!)

In all, a power of attorney or a guardian *must be informed before* making a decision, whether that is approving or disapproving of something medically by the doctor, or financially on behalf of the protected person as a power of attorney or a guardian.

Guardianship & Developmentally Disabled Individuals

Not all people with developmental disabilities need a guardian. **Only if all the professionals agree** that a person **needs** a guardian will a person get one.

*However, just because parents, grandparents on either side of the family, adult brothers and sisters, or any other relatives think or feel that *you* need a guardian, does *not* mean you need one! Only a judge or jury can make that decision/choice!

Unless medical professionals and a judge/jury all agree that you need a guardian, you don't need one!

Understanding Guardianship

Some States offer limited guardianship which allows the protected person to have some say over some parts of their life and the limited guardian to have a final say over other parts of a protected person's life.

One of the roles of a guardian is to include the protected person in making choices as much as possible, such as considering the protected person's wishes and lifestyle. Within knowing that information along with their goals and desires, the guardian helps to enhance and expand the protected person's life, but *makes sure the that person's health is protected.*

Society believes in "safety and health."

On the other hand, there are people in society who like risk and adventure such as skydiving, flying in small airplanes, mountain climbing, horseback riding, etc. Let your guardian know if you have a high-risk personality or if you like any specific "risky activities."

Take reasonable health precautions! **Take responsibility for your own actions!** If I never did scary things like moving out of my parent's house, getting on a commercial airline to fly to another state *with the assistance of my parents and best friend*, or going to college, I would never have grown up mentally, emotionally, or socially!

GUARDIANS MUST NOT "VIEW" OR "USE" THEIR ROLE AS A GUARDIAN TO LIMIT A PERSON'S ACTIVITIES!

Notes

About the Author

Tiffani Harvey was born with multiple physical disabilities and later acquired two more disabilities.

She graduated from high school and completed some college.

When she became an adult, her parents believed other people were using her for their political causes because her parents were never political. She always had to explain to her parents her reasons for her decisions.

She wrote *Growing Independent* to help you understand why you make the decisions you make and to easily answer anybody who should know why you made those decisions.

Examples of who should know are your emotionally close family, your professional team, a couple of very close friends, and anyone a professional or a trusted family member approves of.

If this book has helped you in any way, please write a review or send feedback to Tiffani Harvey at responsiblyindependent@yahoo.com.

www.ingramcontent.com/pod-product-compliance
Lightning Source LLC
Chambersburg PA
CBHW071405120626
46546CB00002B/819